Brave Wings

Rise. Dream. Live.

A Coloring Book to Celebrate & Empower Women

by April McCallum

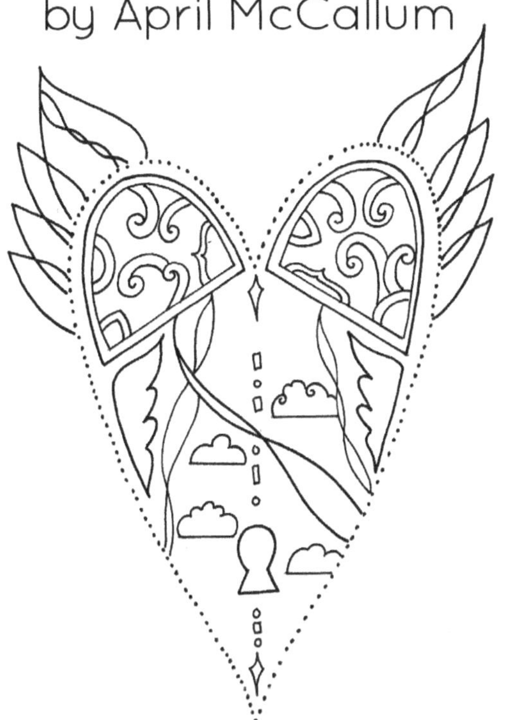

ISBN-13: 978-1-7325752-5-7

Brave Wings: A Coloring Book to Celebrate & Empower Women

Published in the United States by Heart & Key Publishing

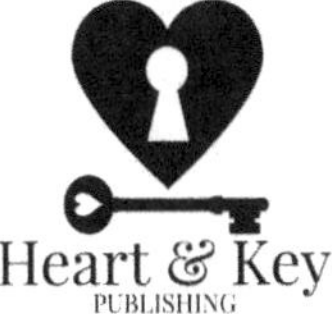

Cover Design Collaboration and Colorization by Pete Berg

www.aprilmccallumdesigns.com

Welcome!

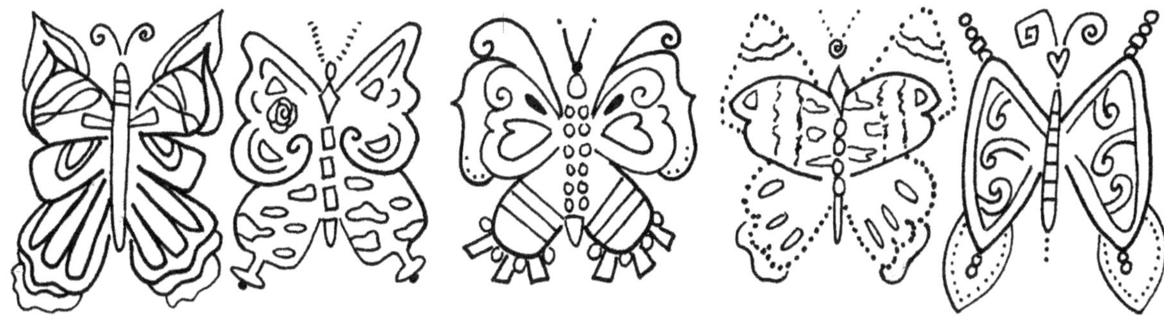

Hello Beautiful.

Art and Heart... This collection of coloring pages was created with love, just for you. A powerful combination of beautiful hand-drawn illustrations, verses, thoughts and quotes to inspire you to rise, dream and live more fully.

Brave Wings is a coloring book, but it is also a message for women — a love letter to their hearts. The world needs more women who've discovered their life's purpose and passionately pursue it. Women who refuse to allow their fears, other's words, the past, or their weaknesses to define or confine them. Women who are strong *and* vulnerable, yet free. Women who love and are loved. Ones who will dance to the beat of their own uniqueness while using their gifts to lift others. Ones who don't limit themselves to mediocrity, rather embrace and celebrate and honor life to the fullest. Ones who dare to dream and create. Ones who are wise with their hearts, heads and hands. And ones who purpose to make the world a better and more beautiful place. They are lifters, builders, protectors, inspirers, forerunners, lovers and warriors. Warriors of love and grace, peace and hope, substance and destiny. They are brave {even when their knees are weak.} They step up. They endure. They conquer. They shine. They thrive. And they help others do the same. Take courage. Spread your wings.

> *"A caterpillar is awesome, but if the caterpillar stopped there — if she just decided that good is good enough — we would all miss out on the beautiful creature she would become." — Rachel Hollis*

Tips: You will notice a bit of extra margin on the binding side. I intentionally designed it that way for ease of maneuvering. If you would like to practice your lines and coloring tools, you will find a blank page in the back of the book to do just that. If you plan to use non-dry coloring materials, please place a blank sheet or two under the page you're coloring so it doesn't bleed through. Consider this book a place for you to soak in color and positivity and to saturate yourself in intention and possibility.

Rise. Dream. Live!

XO April

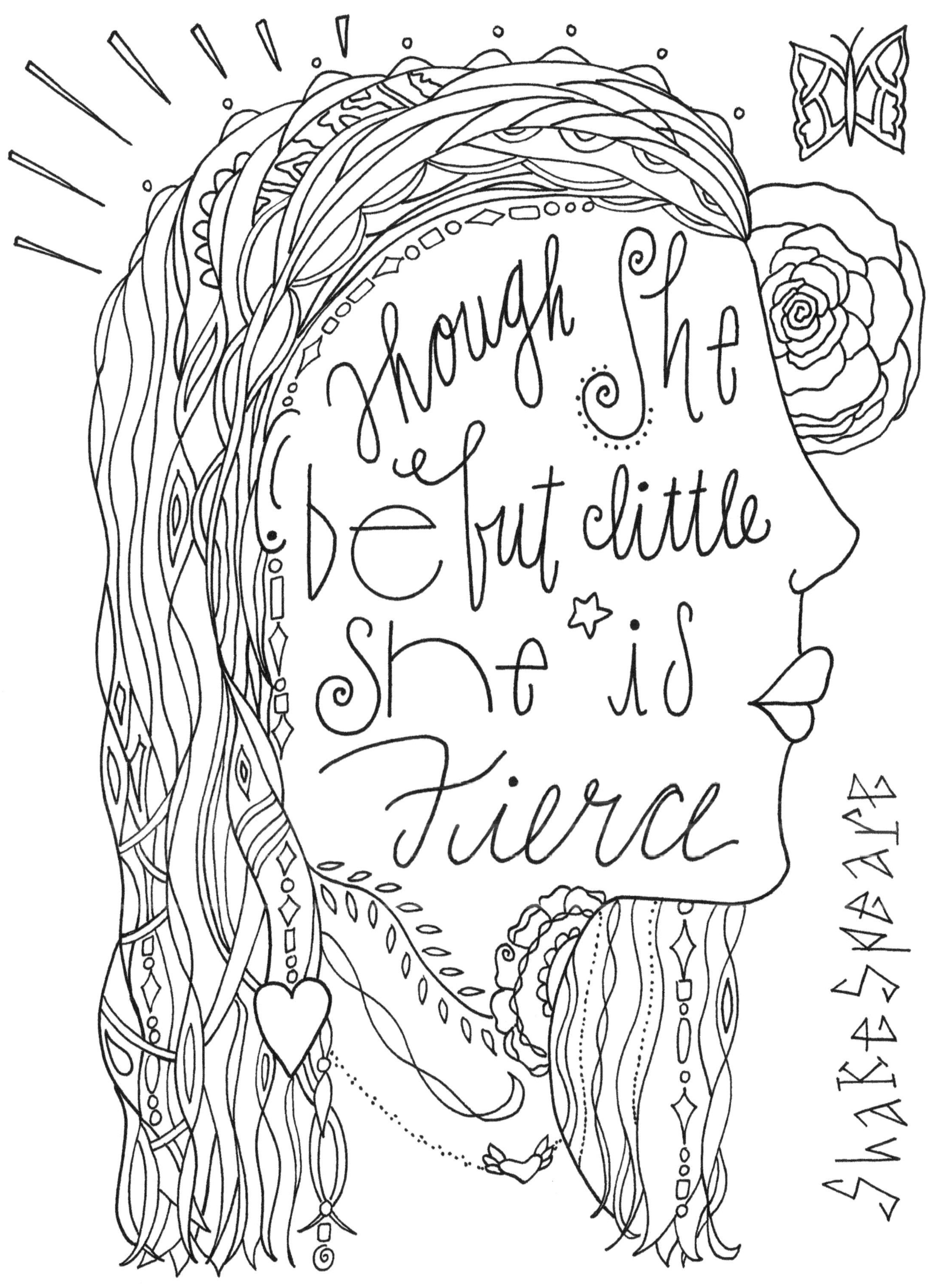
Though She
be but little
She is
Fierce
SHAKESPEARE

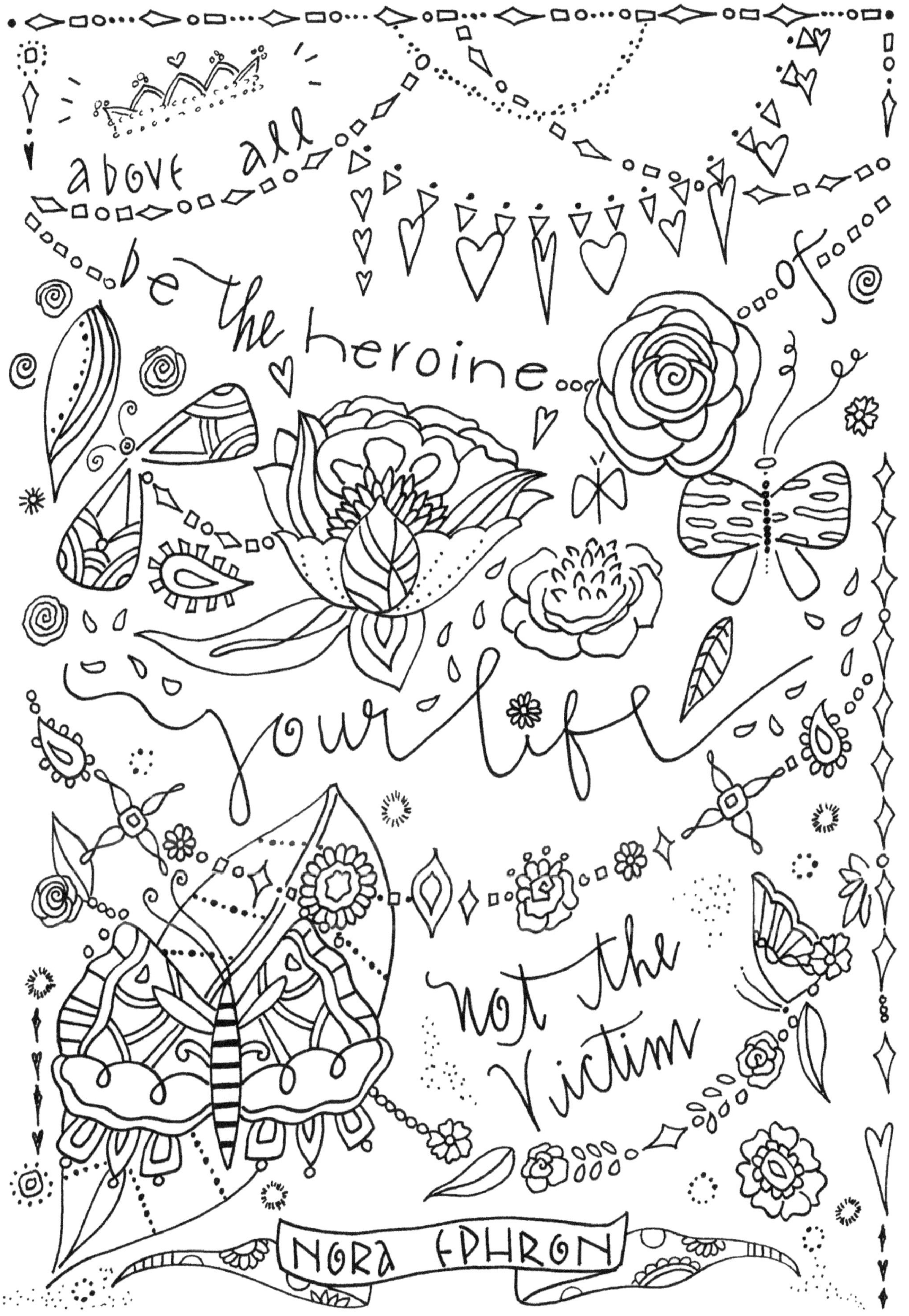
above all
be the heroine of
your life
not the
victim
NORA EPHRON

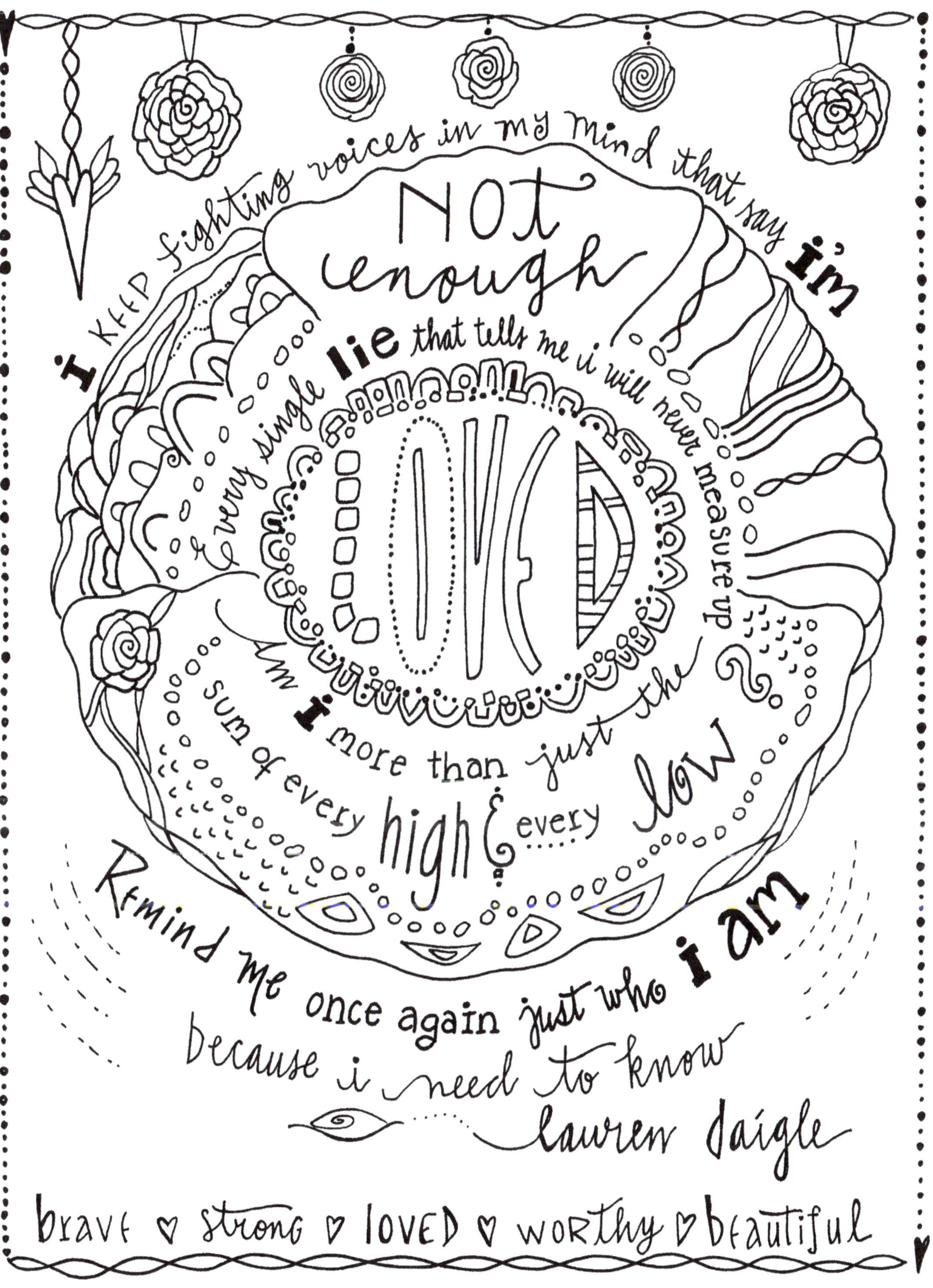
i keep fighting voices in my mind that say i'm
NOT enough
every single lie that tells me i will never measure up
Am i more than just the sum of every high & every low
LOVED
Remind me once again just who i am
because i need to know
lauren daigle
brave ♡ strong ♡ loved ♡ worthy ♡ beautiful

One step at a time

one
one
one
ONE
one
one
1
one
one
one
one
ONE one
one
One
one
one
ONE
one

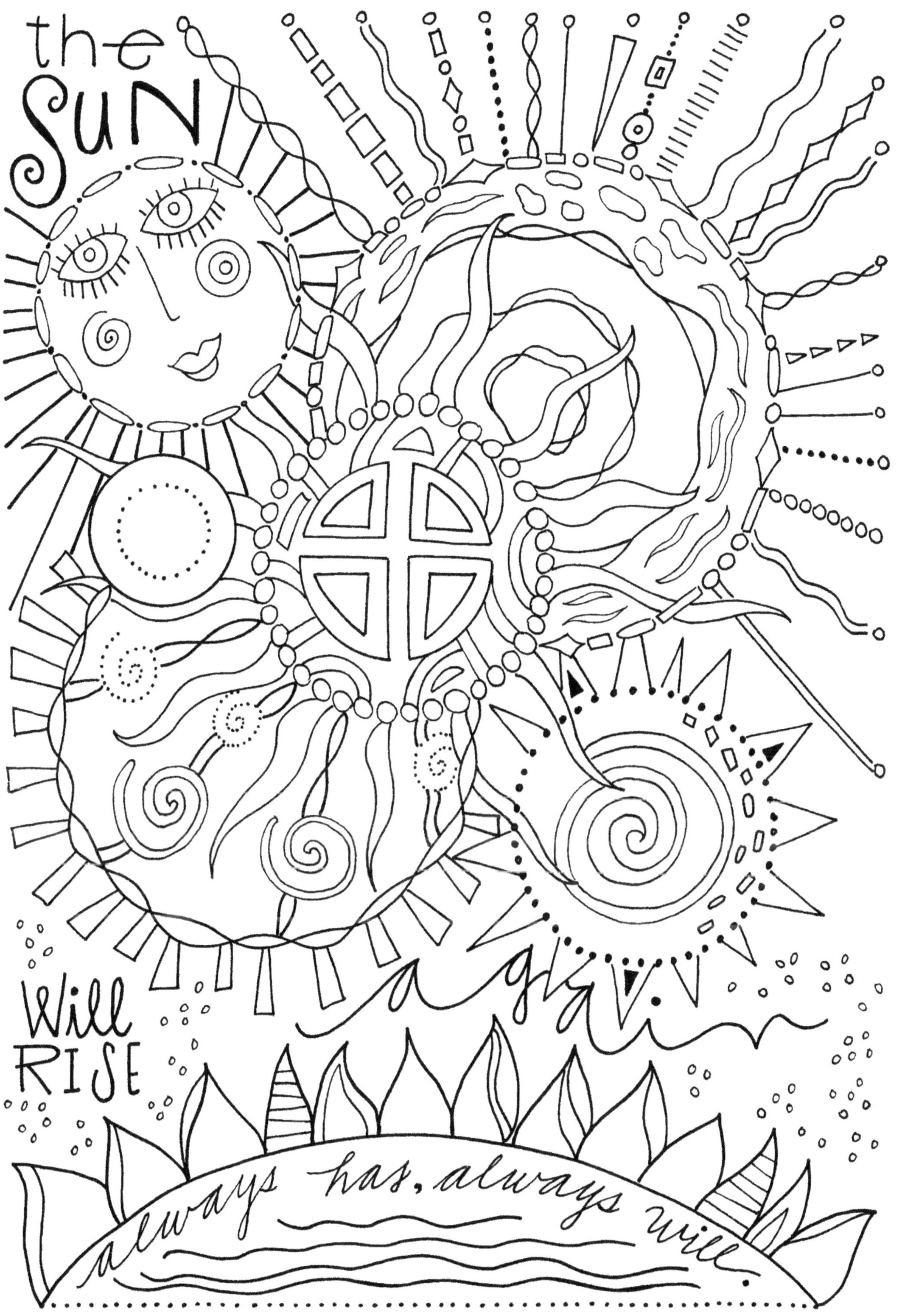
the Sun
Will RISE
again
always has, always will.

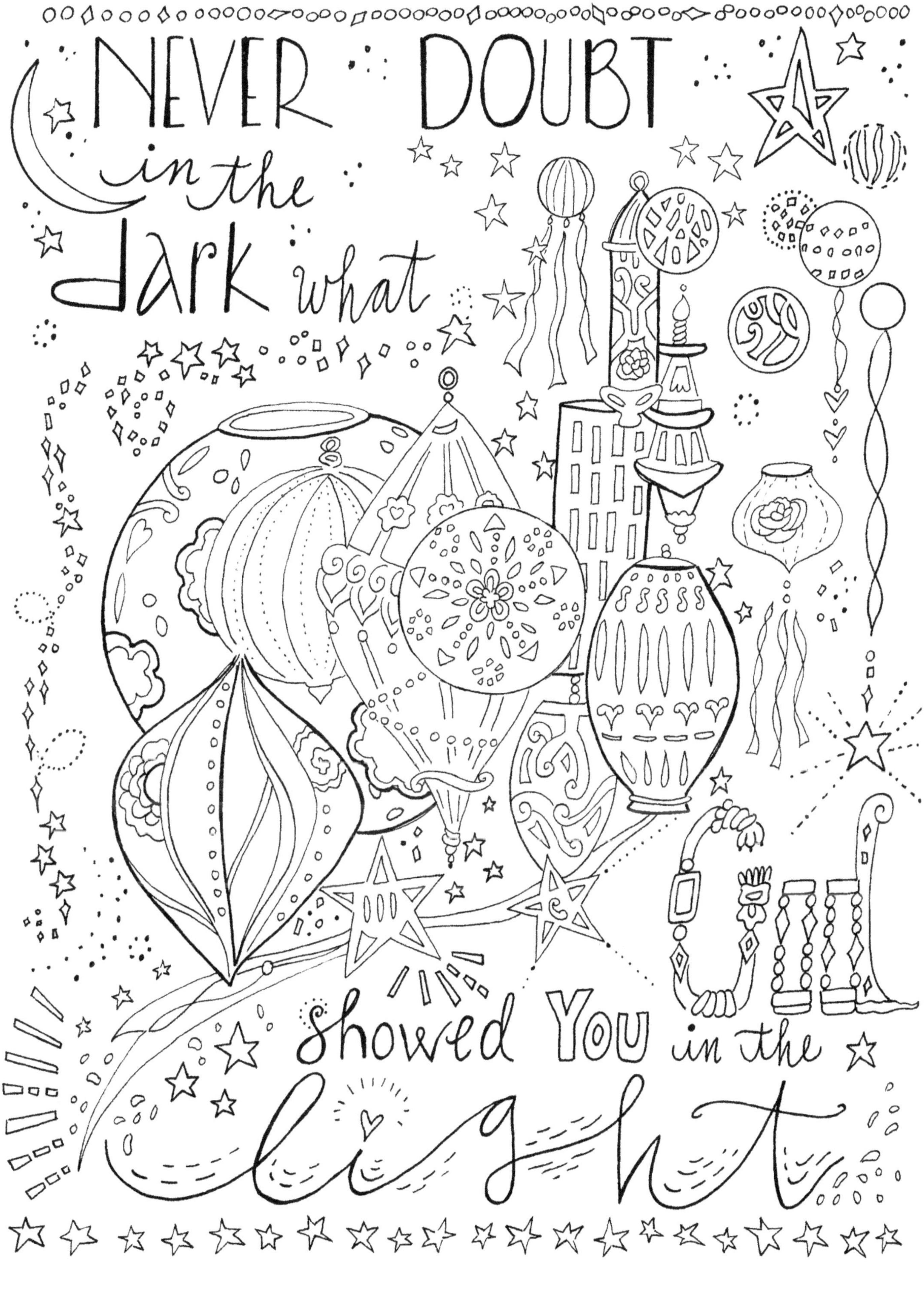

NEVER DOUBT in the dark what God showed YOU in the light

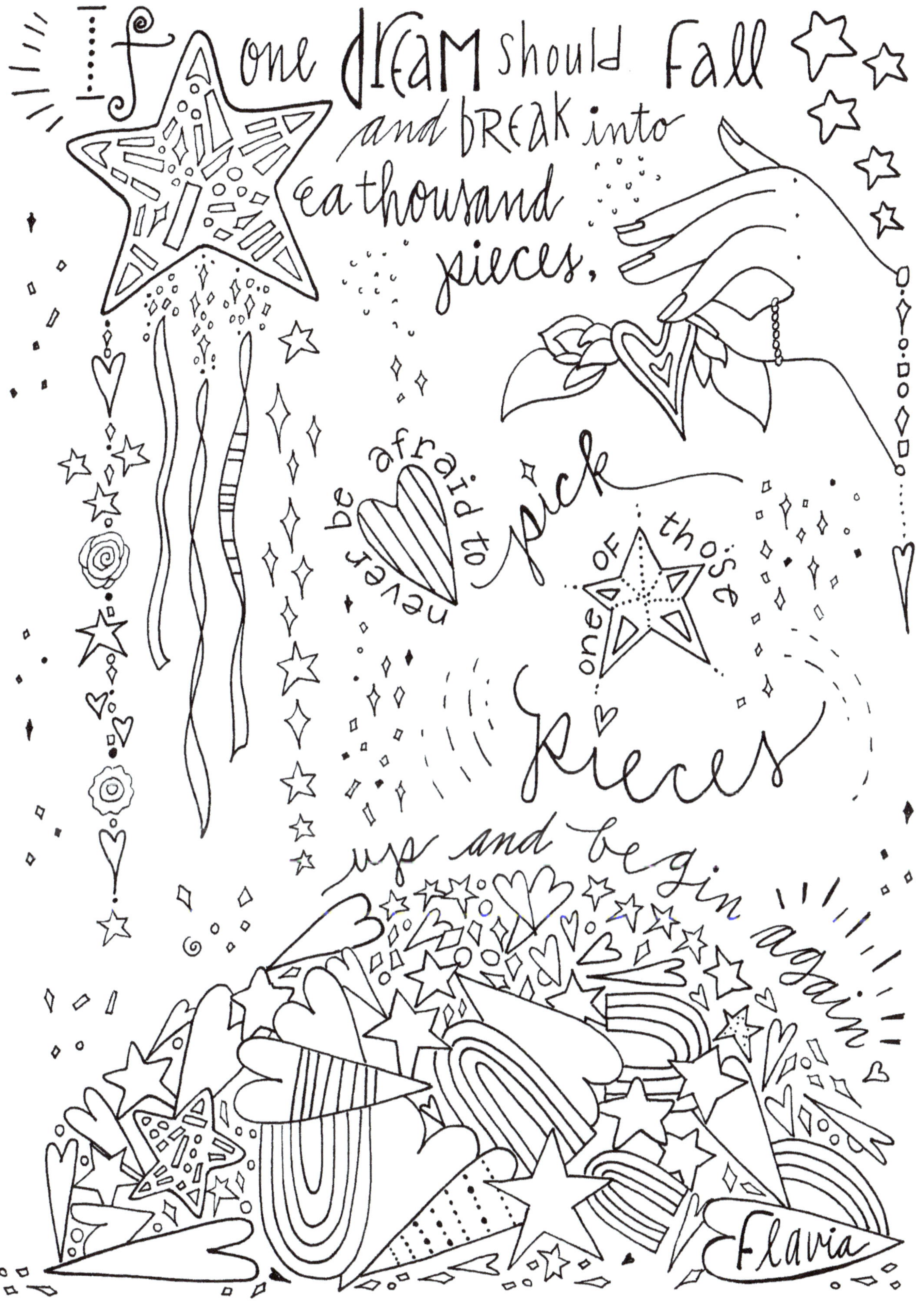
If one dream should fall
and break into
a thousand
pieces,
never be afraid to pick
one of those
pieces
up and begin again
Flavia

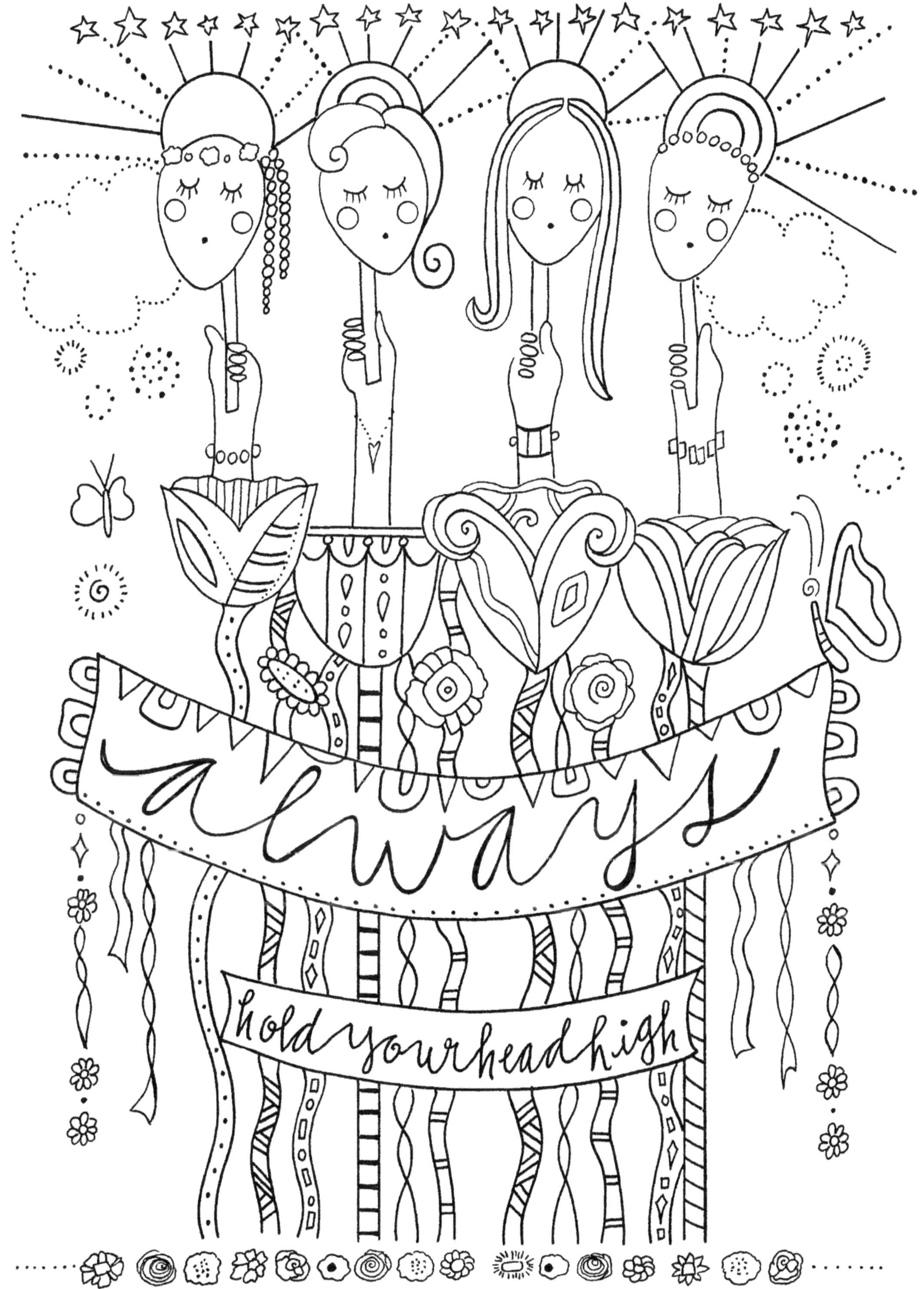
always
hold your head high

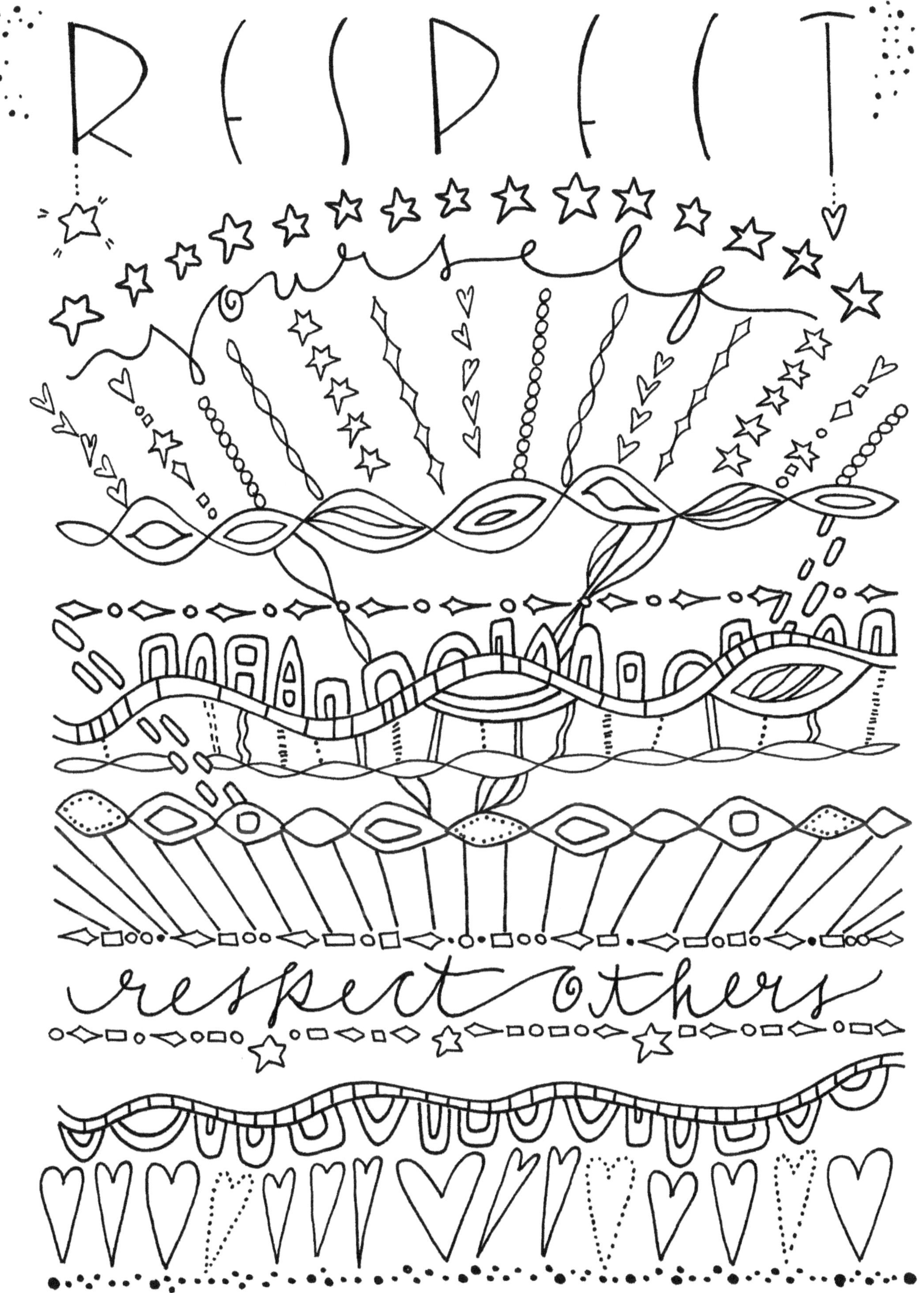
RESPECT
yourself
respect others

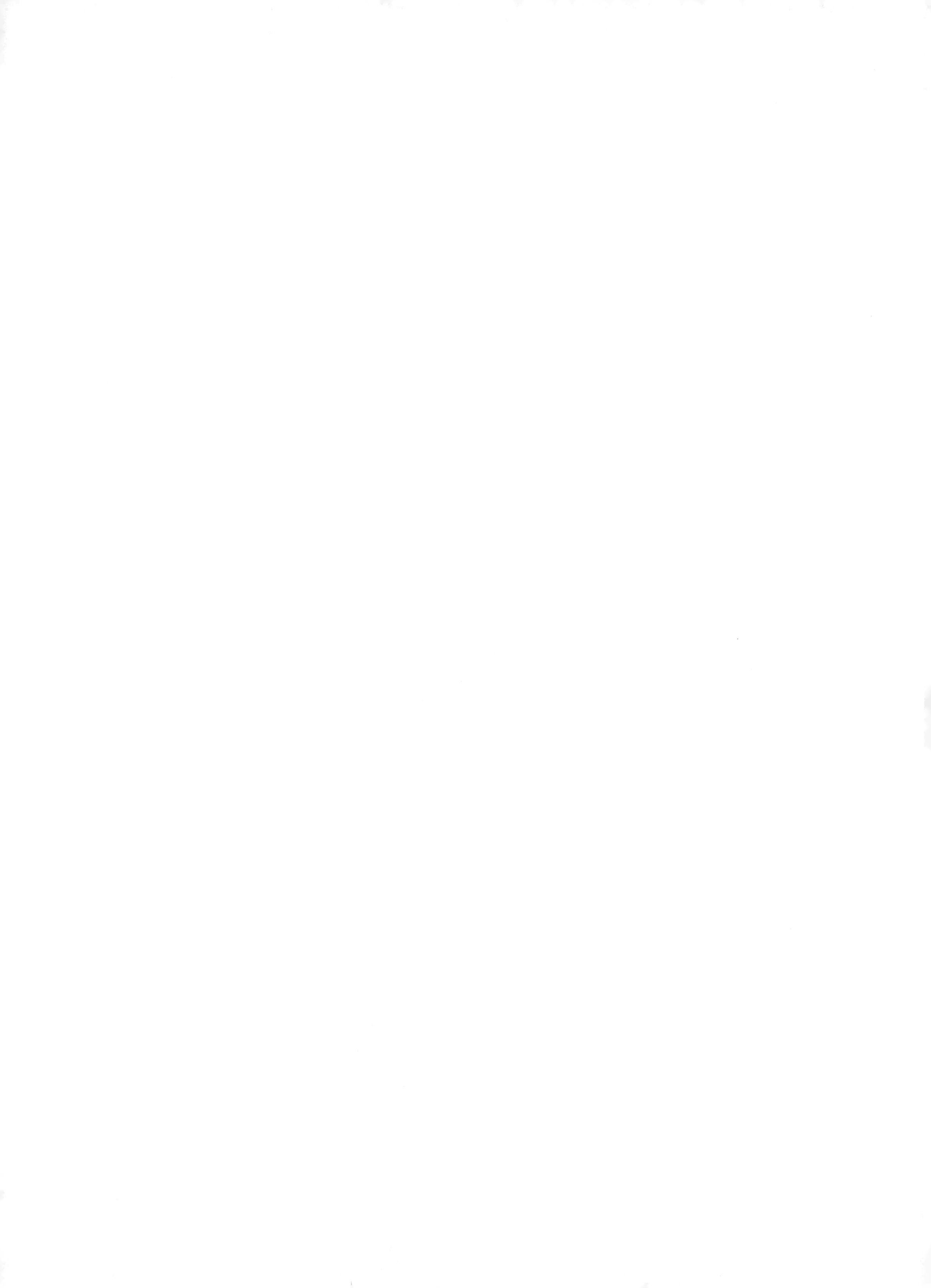

YOU MAY NOT CONTROL ALL THE

events that happen to you

but YOU CAN DECIDE

NOT TO BE REDUCED BY THEM.

Maya Angelou

Never allow ANYONE to STEAL your

JOY joy joy

JOY

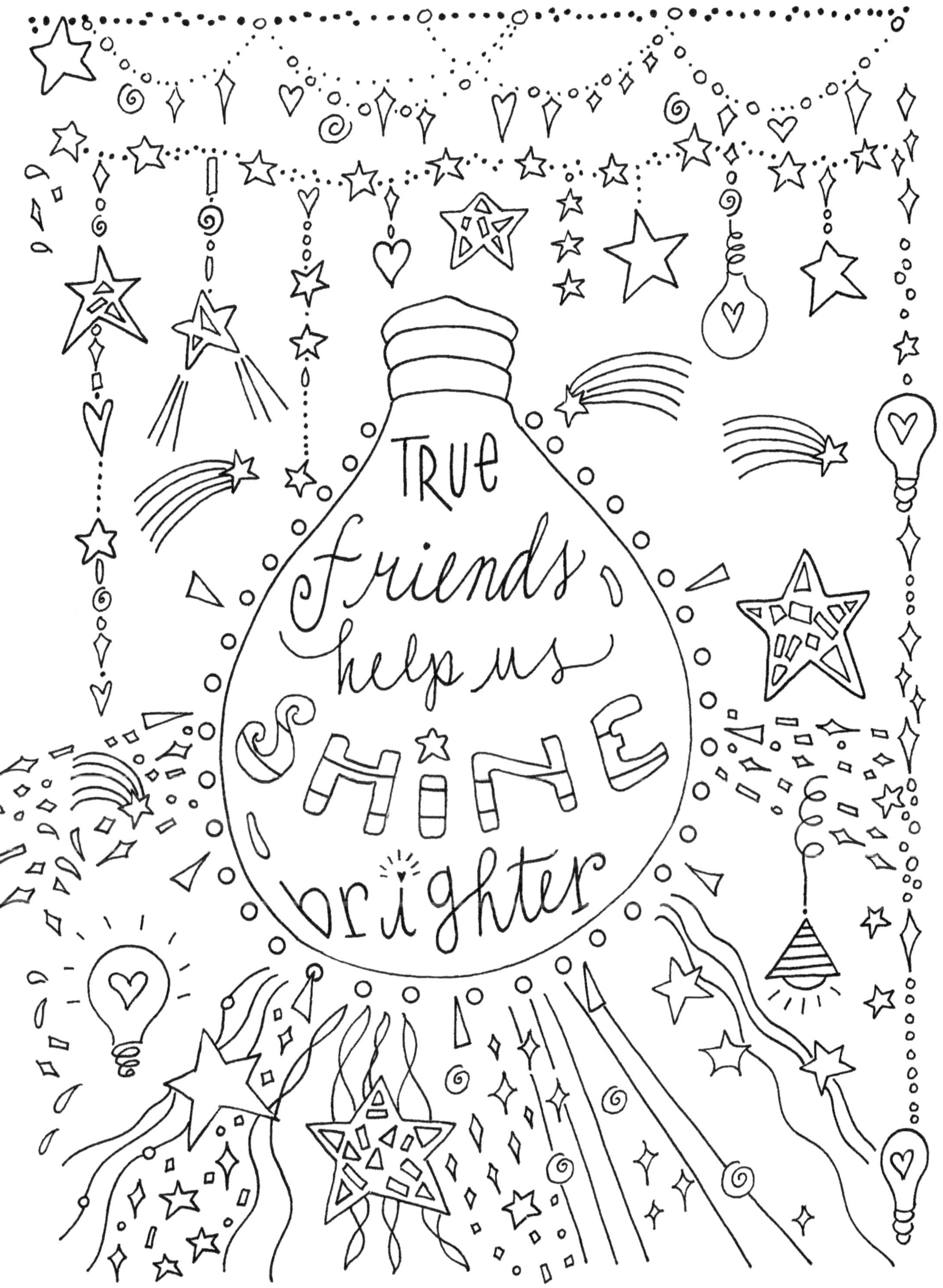
True
friends
help us
SHINE
brighter

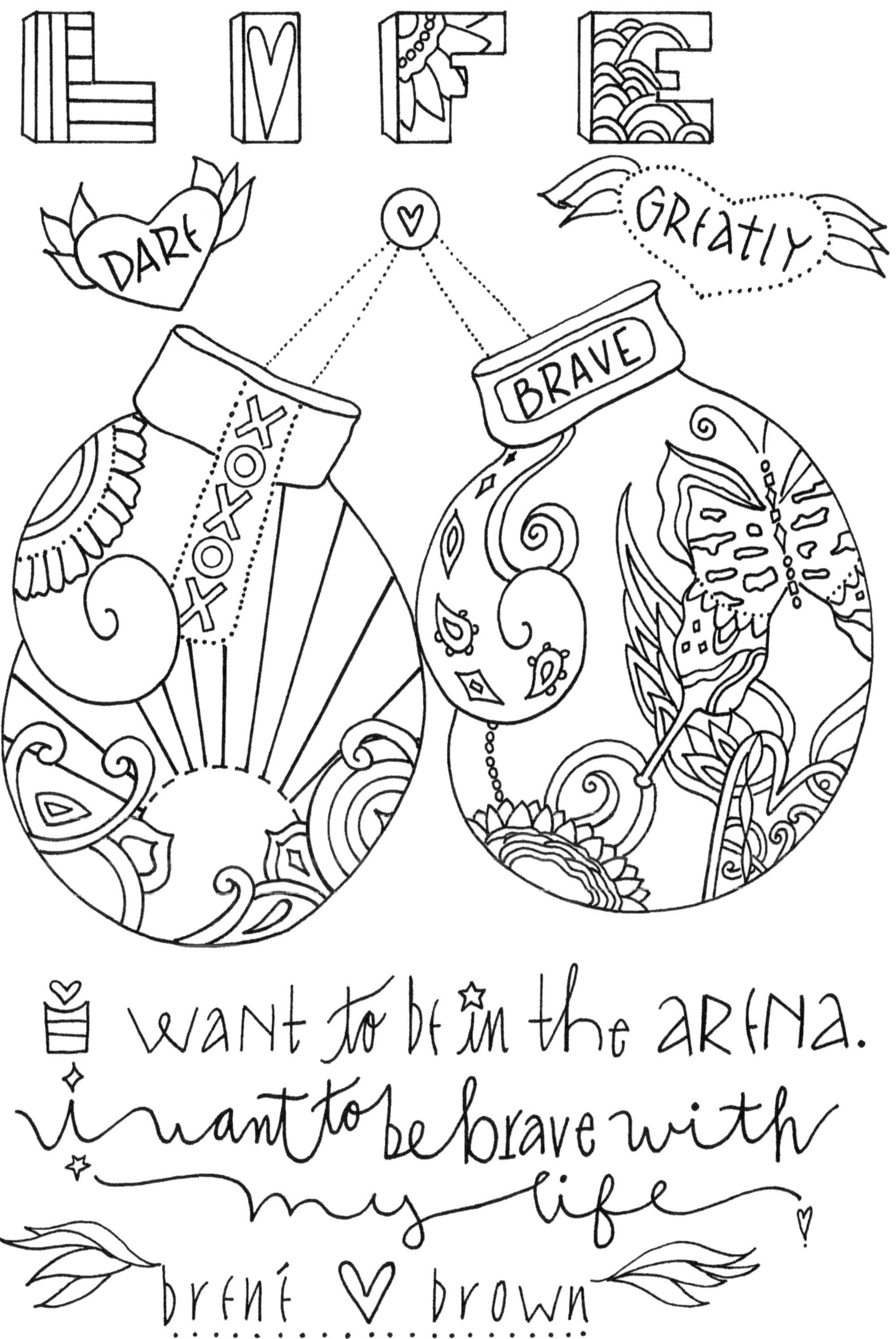
LIFE
DARE
GREATLY
BRAVE
XOXOXOX
I want to be in the arena.
i want to be brave with my life
brené brown

Nevermind searching for who you are.

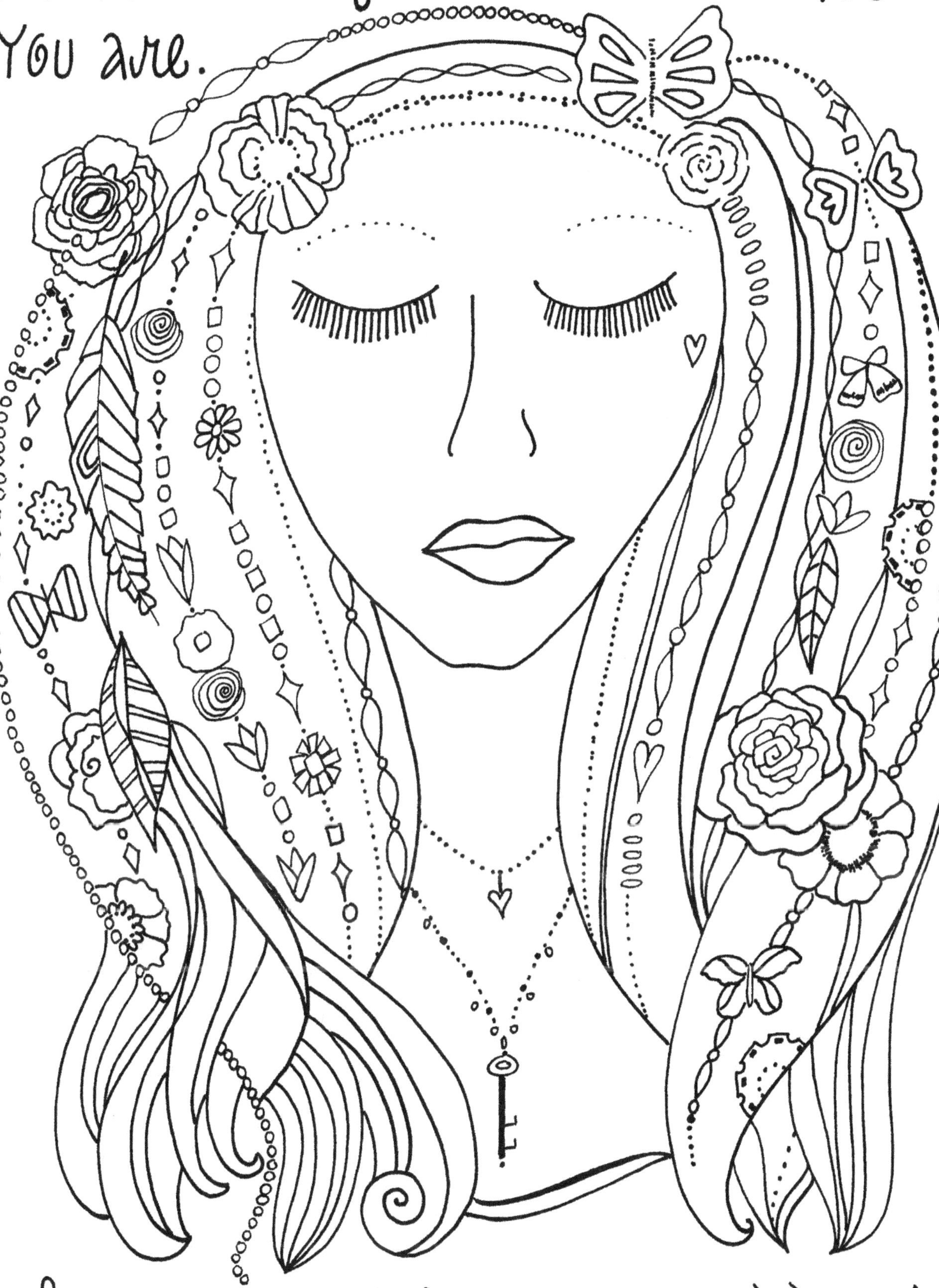

Search for the person you aspire to be.

Robert Brault

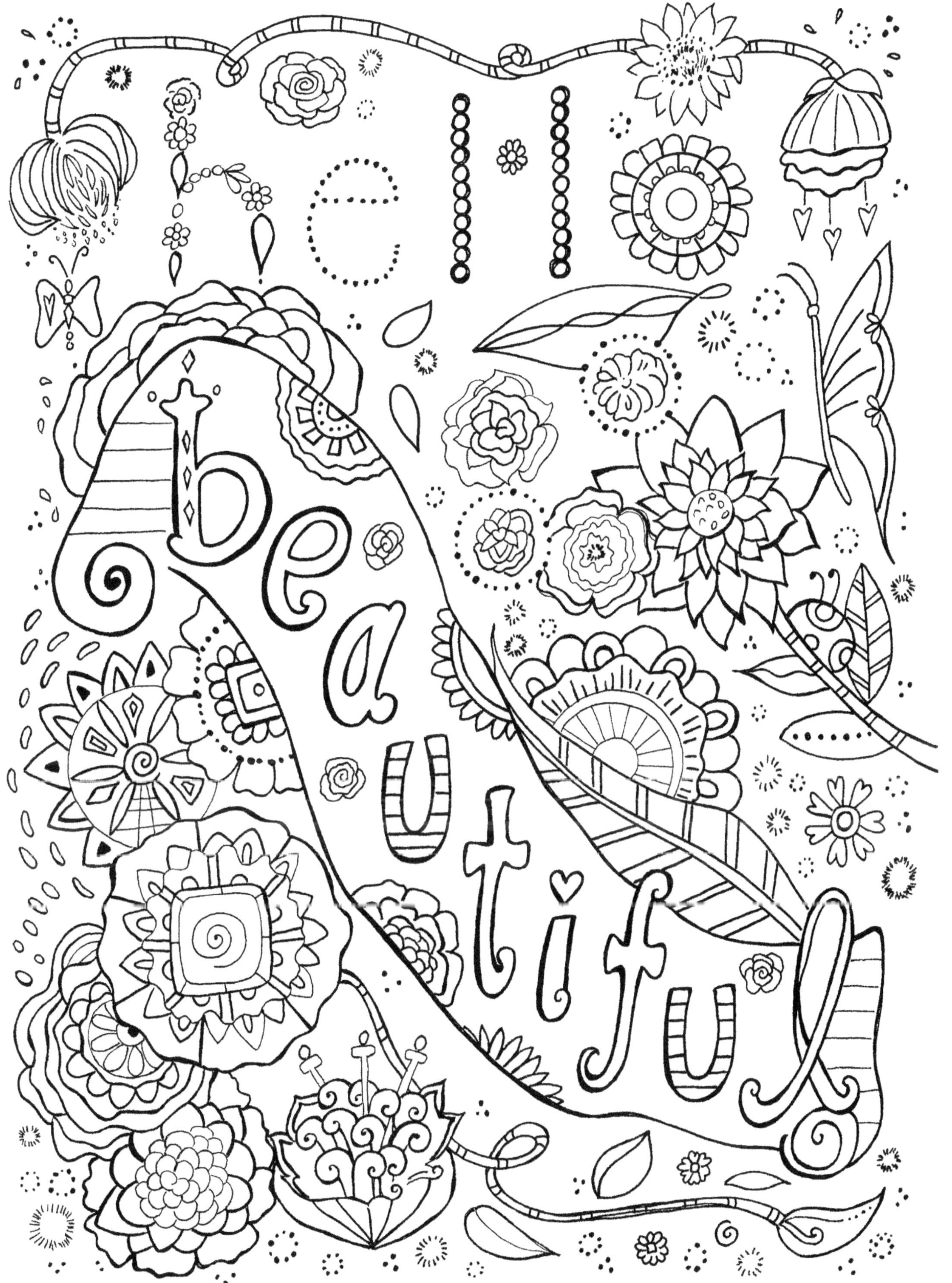
hello
beautiful

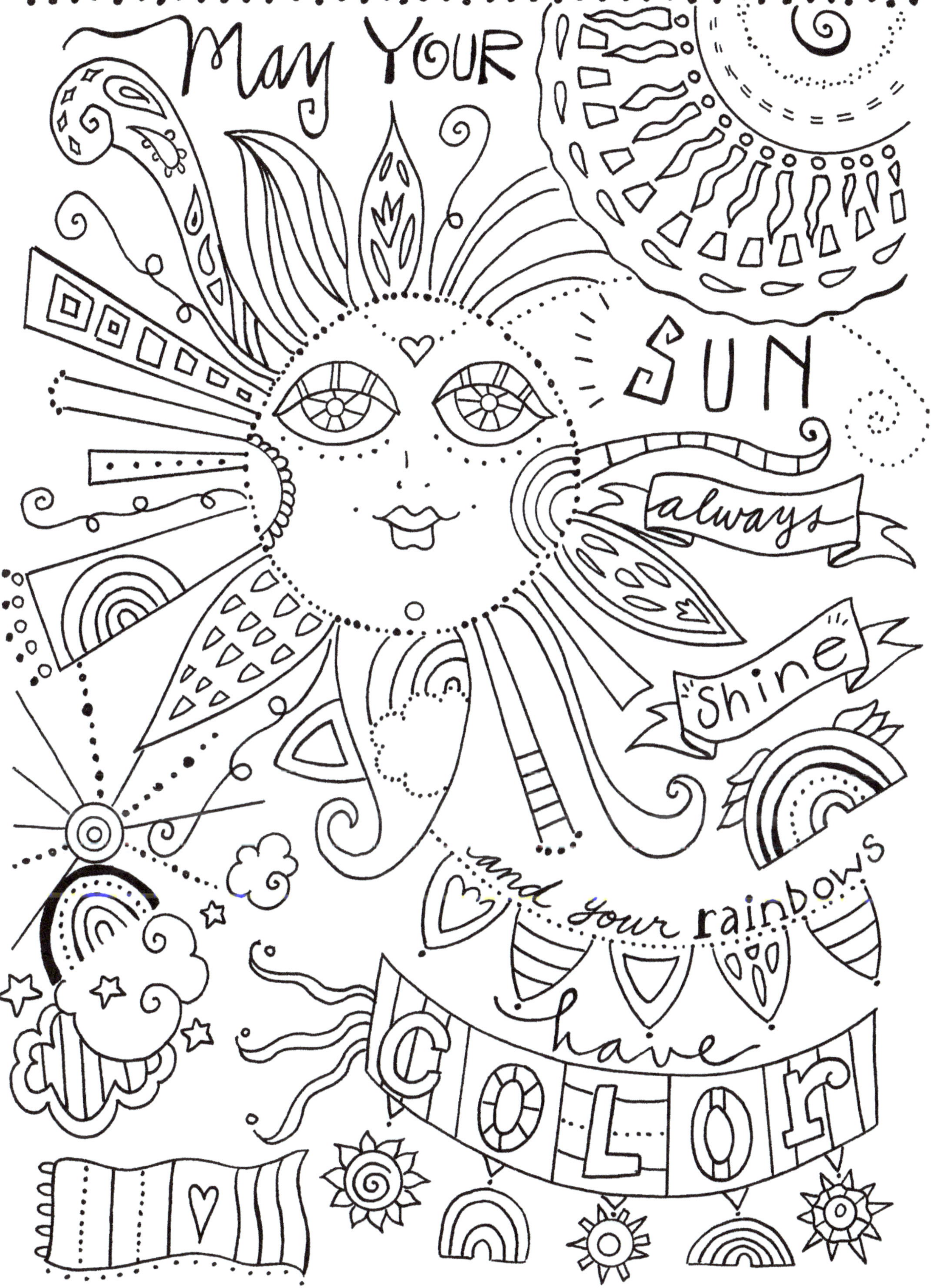
May YOUR
SUN
always
Shine
and your rainbows
have
COLOR

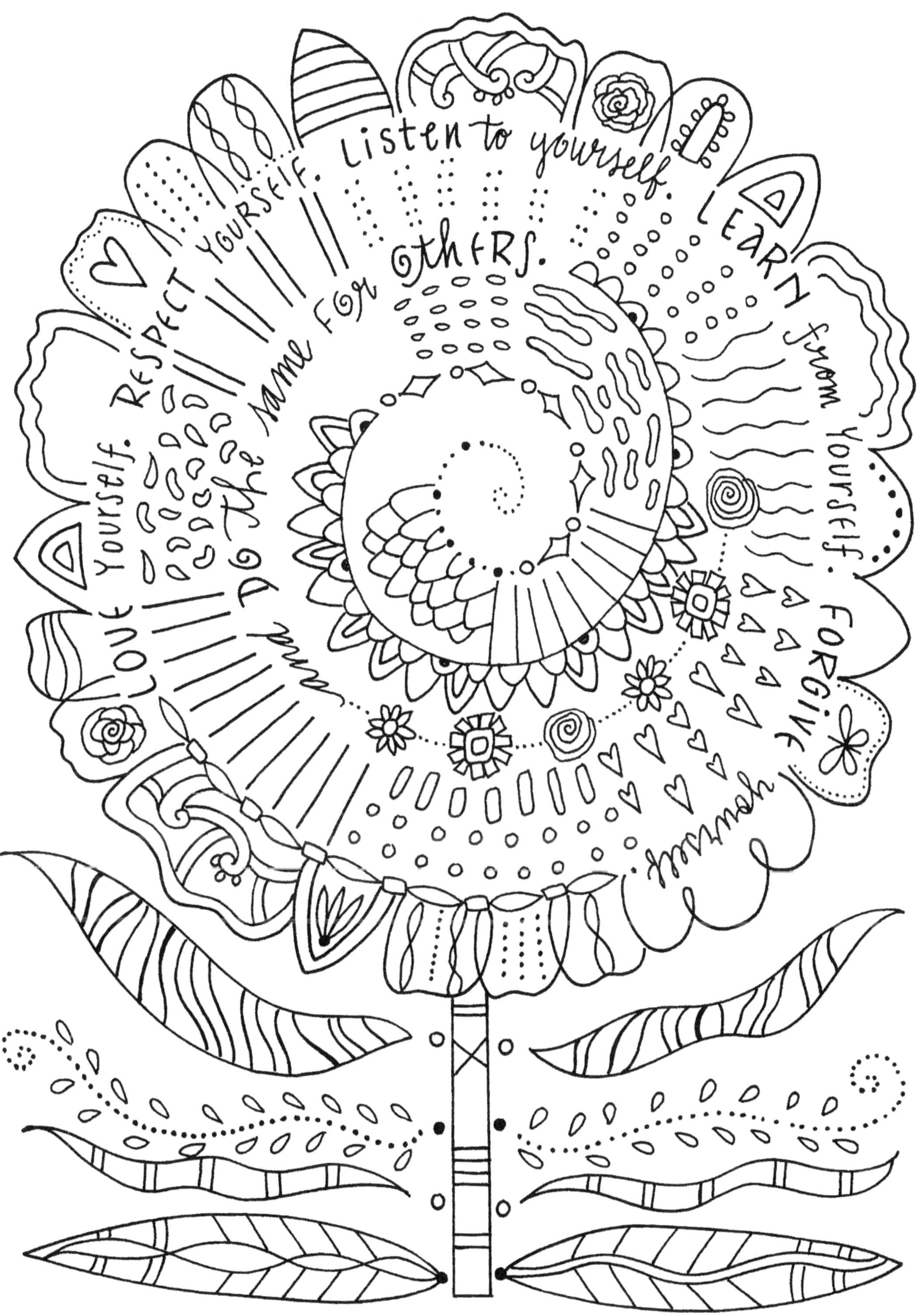
Love yourself. Respect yourself. Listen to yourself. Learn from yourself. Forgive yourself
and Do the same for others.

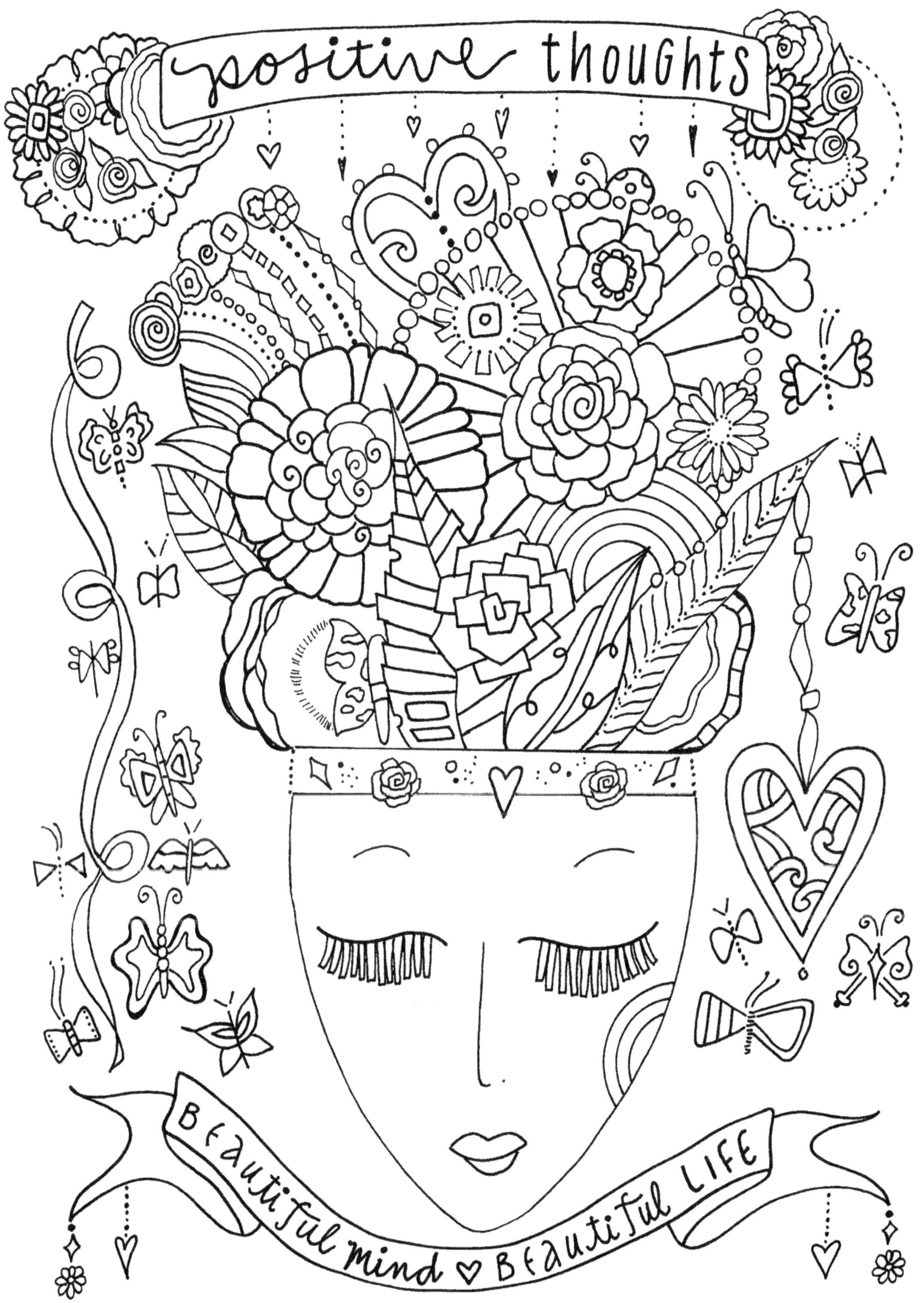
positive thoughts
Beautiful mind ♡ Beautiful LIFE

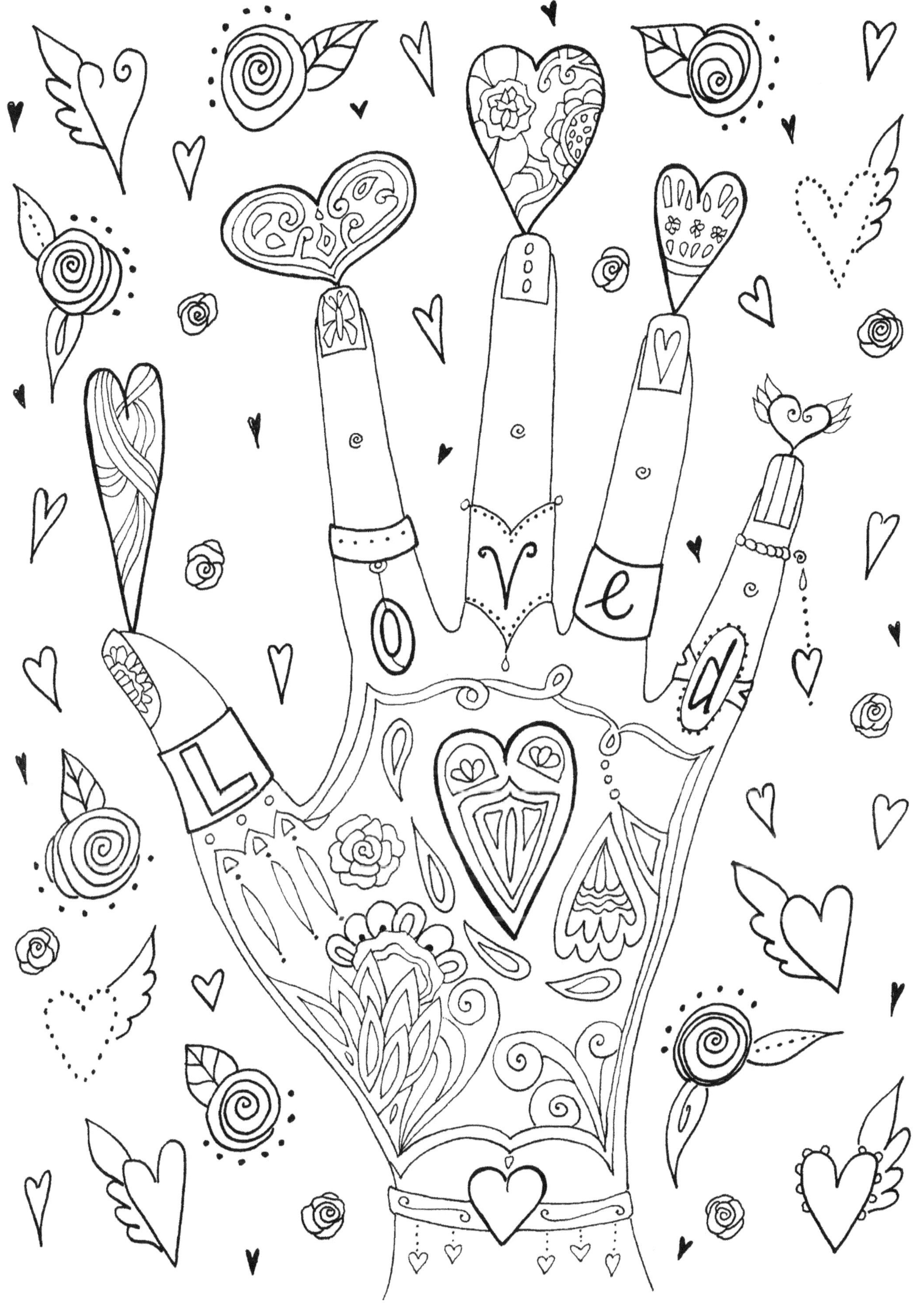
Loved

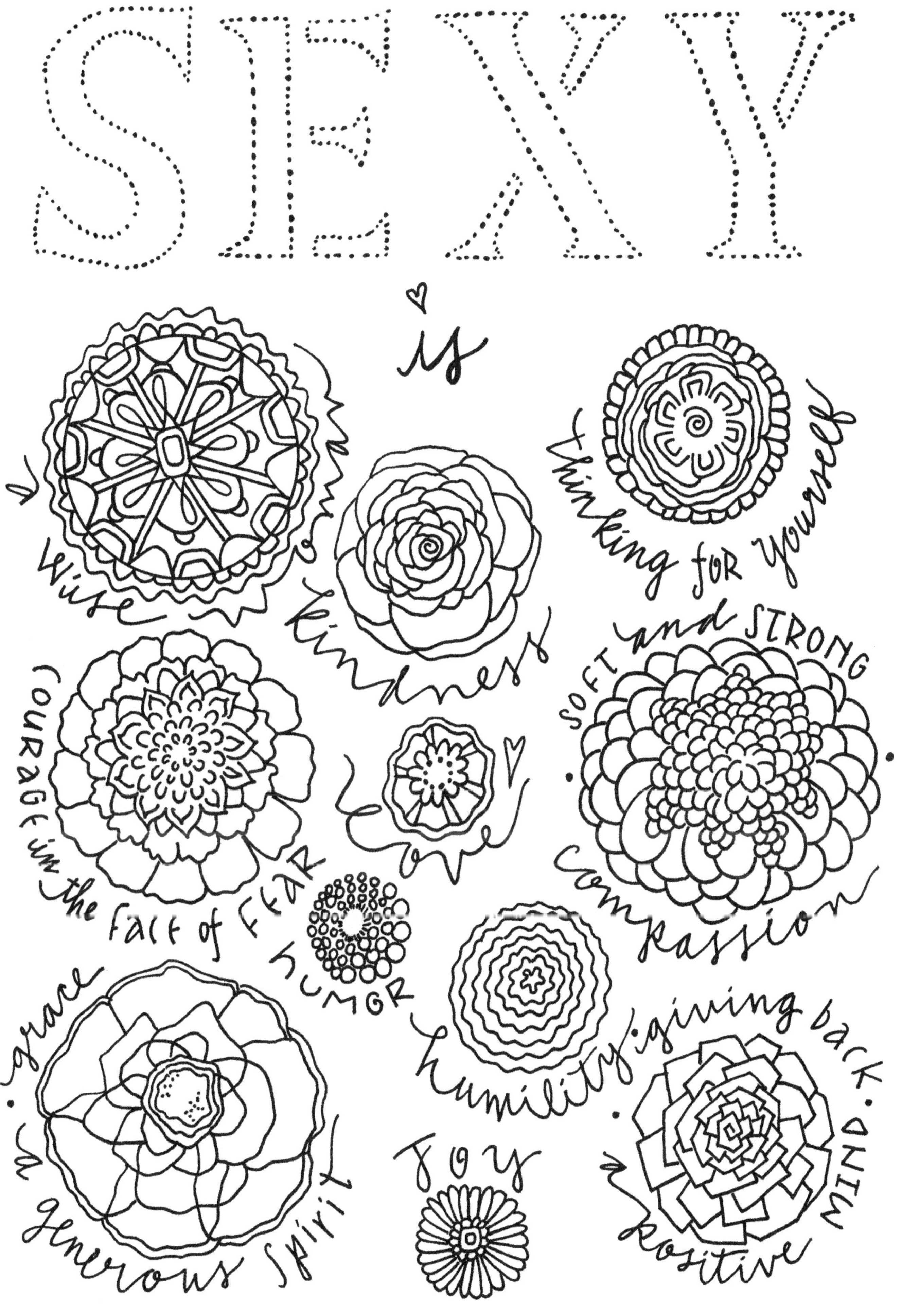
SEXY
is
a wise woman
kindness
thinking for yourself
soft and STRONG
compassion
COURAGE in the face of FEAR
love
HUMOR
humility
giving back
grace
a generous spirit
JOY
a positive MIND

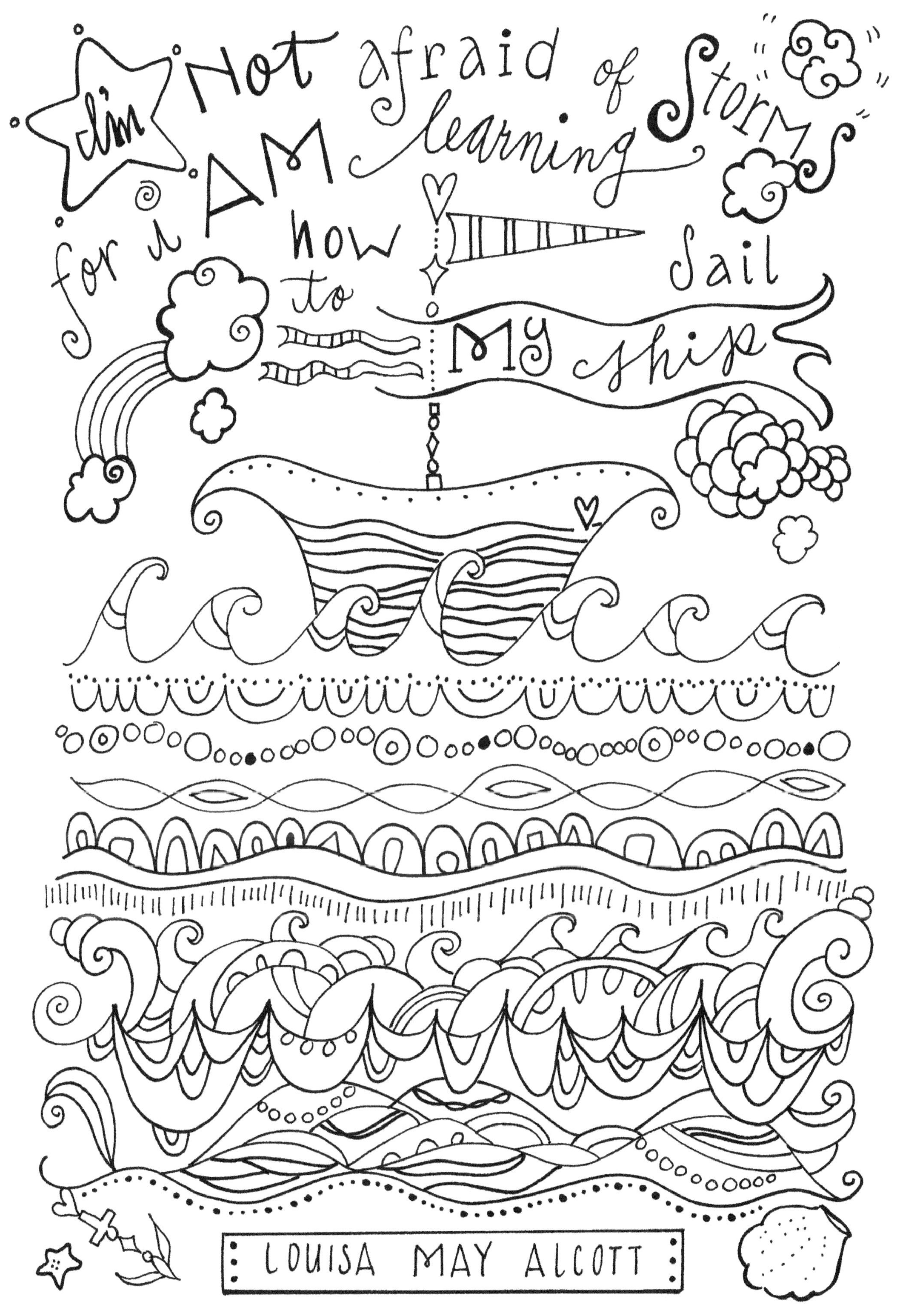
I'm Not afraid of Storms
for I AM learning how to sail My ship
LOUISA MAY ALCOTT

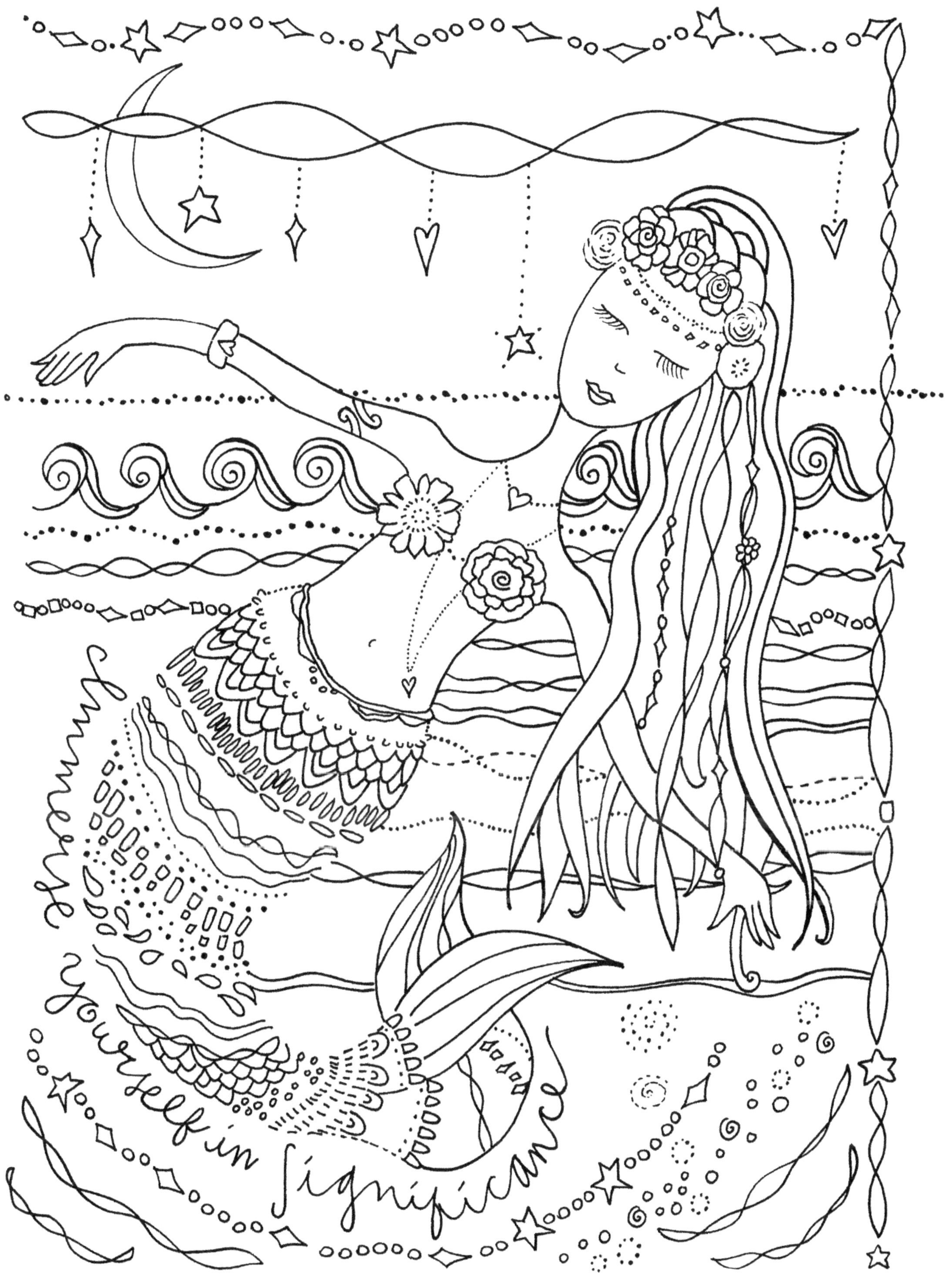
Immerse yourself in significance

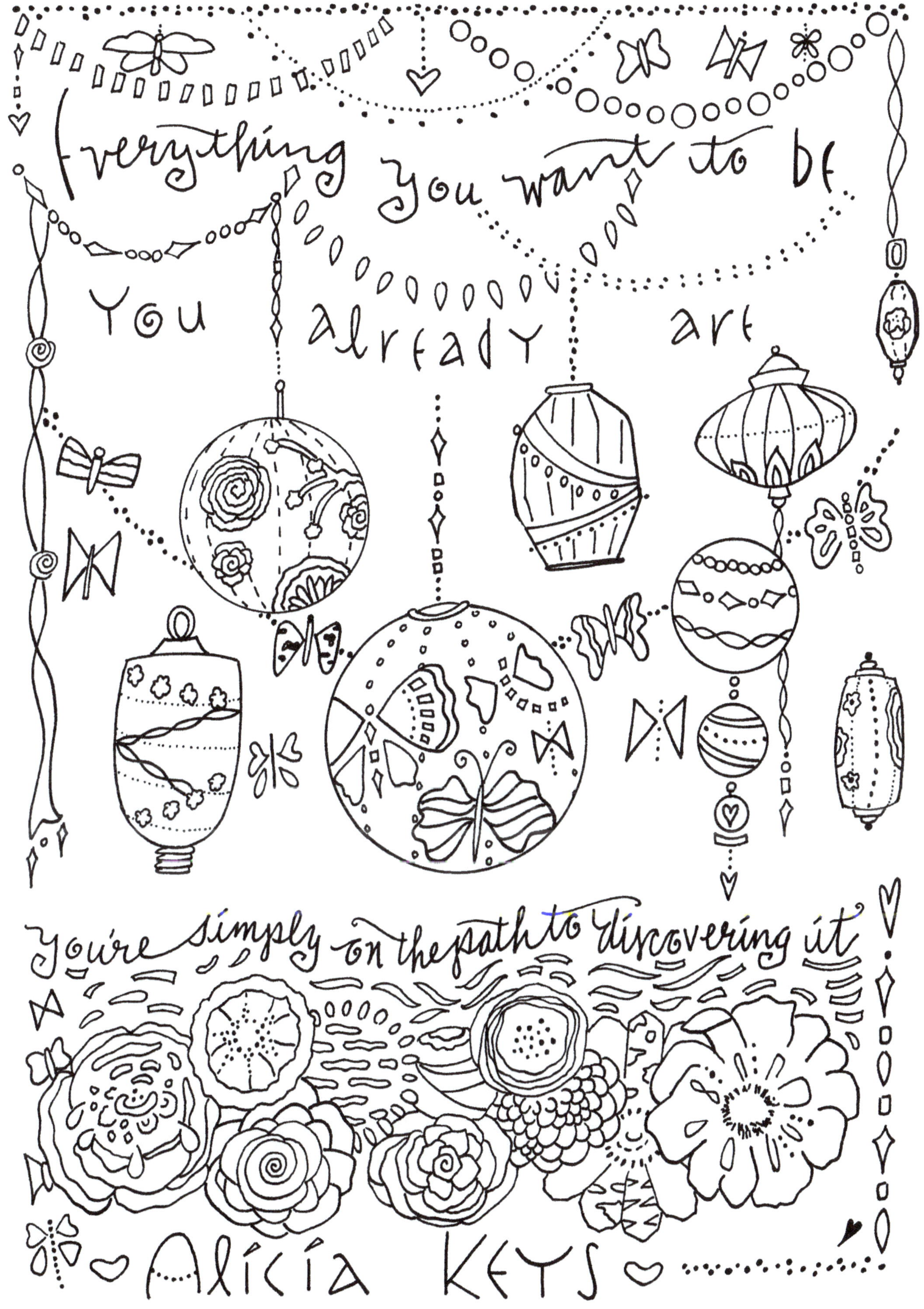
Everything you want to be
you already are
You're simply on the path to discovering it
Alicia Keys

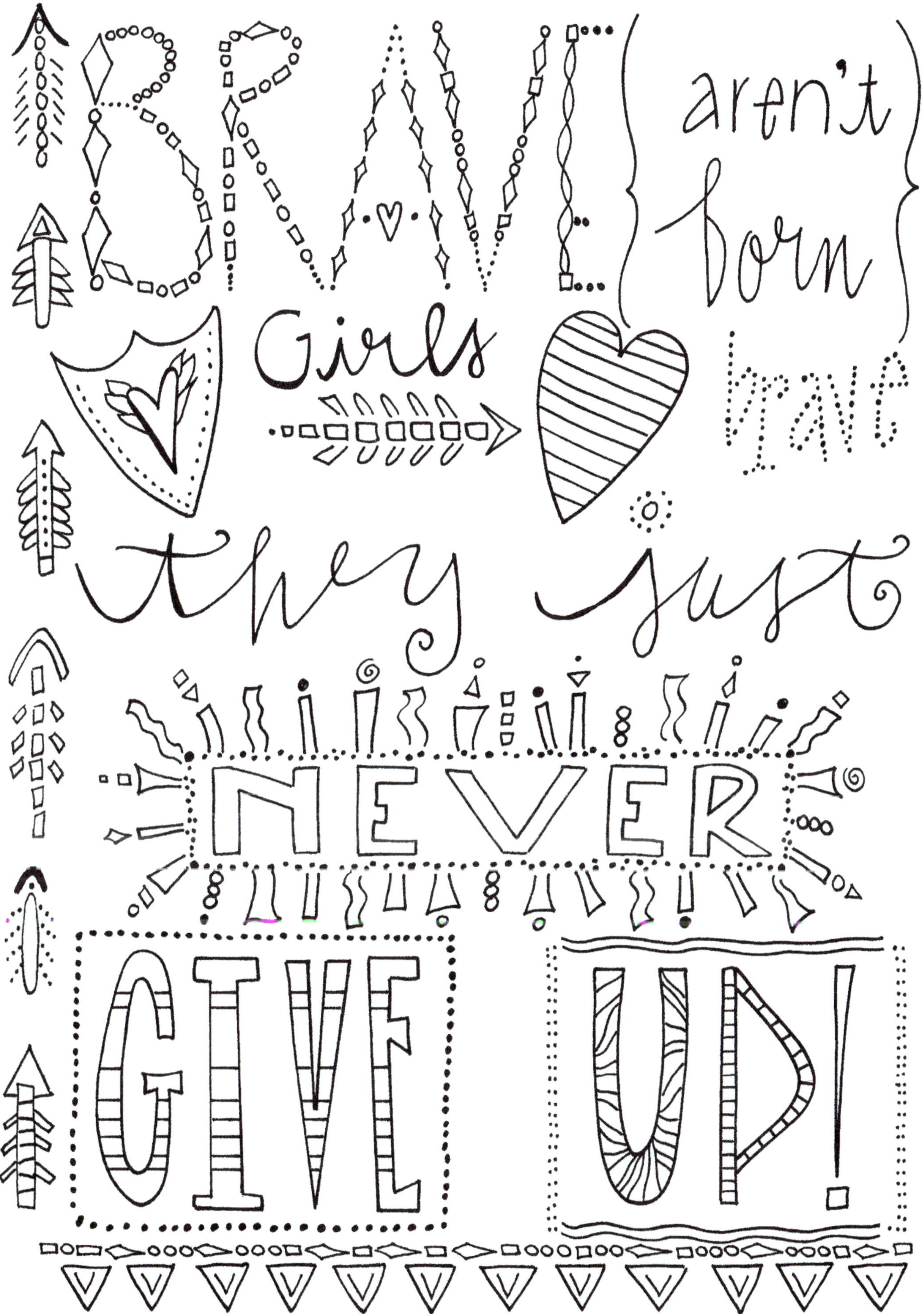
BRAVE
(aren't born)
Girls
brave
they just
NEVER
GIVE UP!

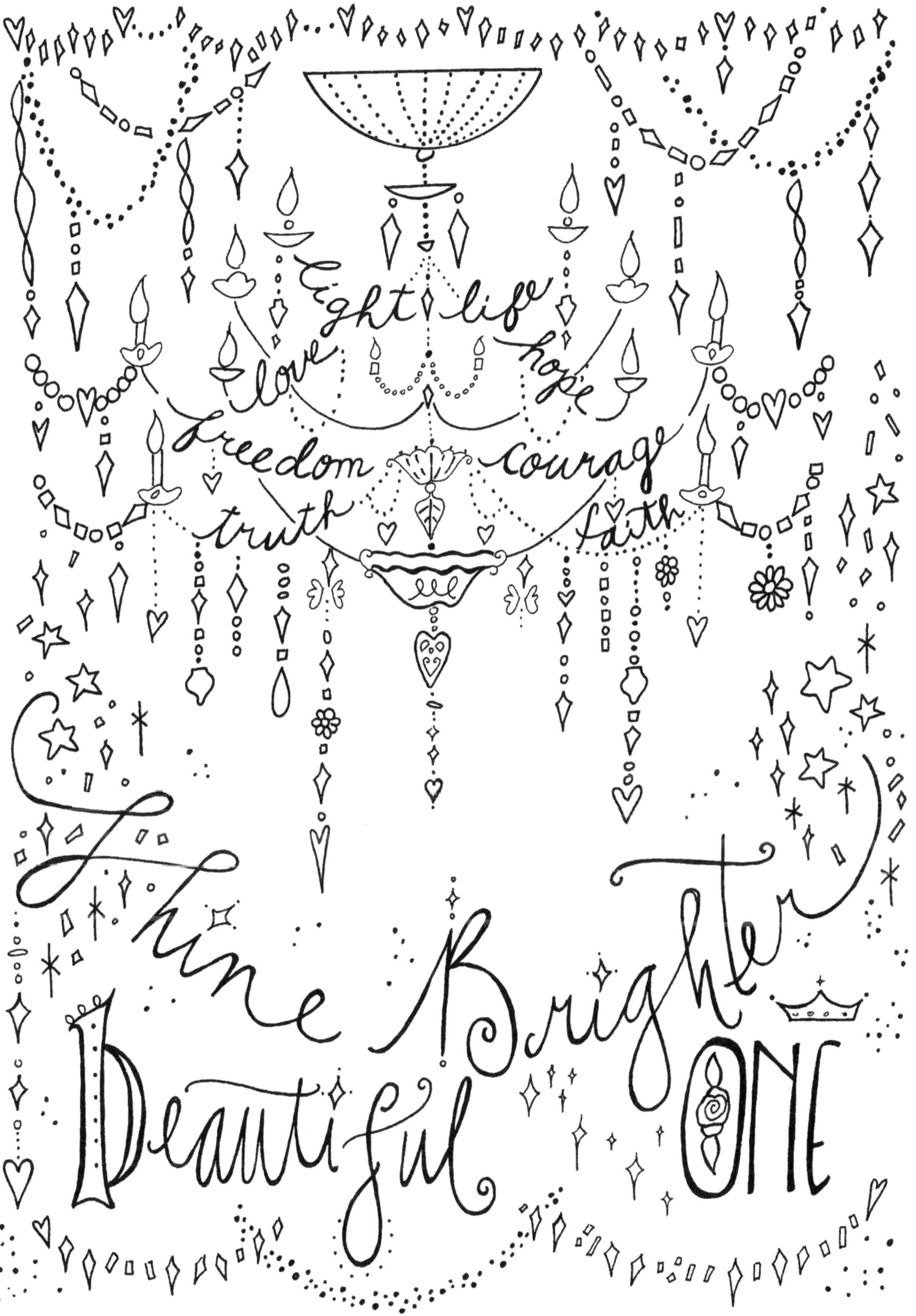
light
life
love
hope
freedom
courag
truth
faith
Shine Brighter
Beautiful ONE

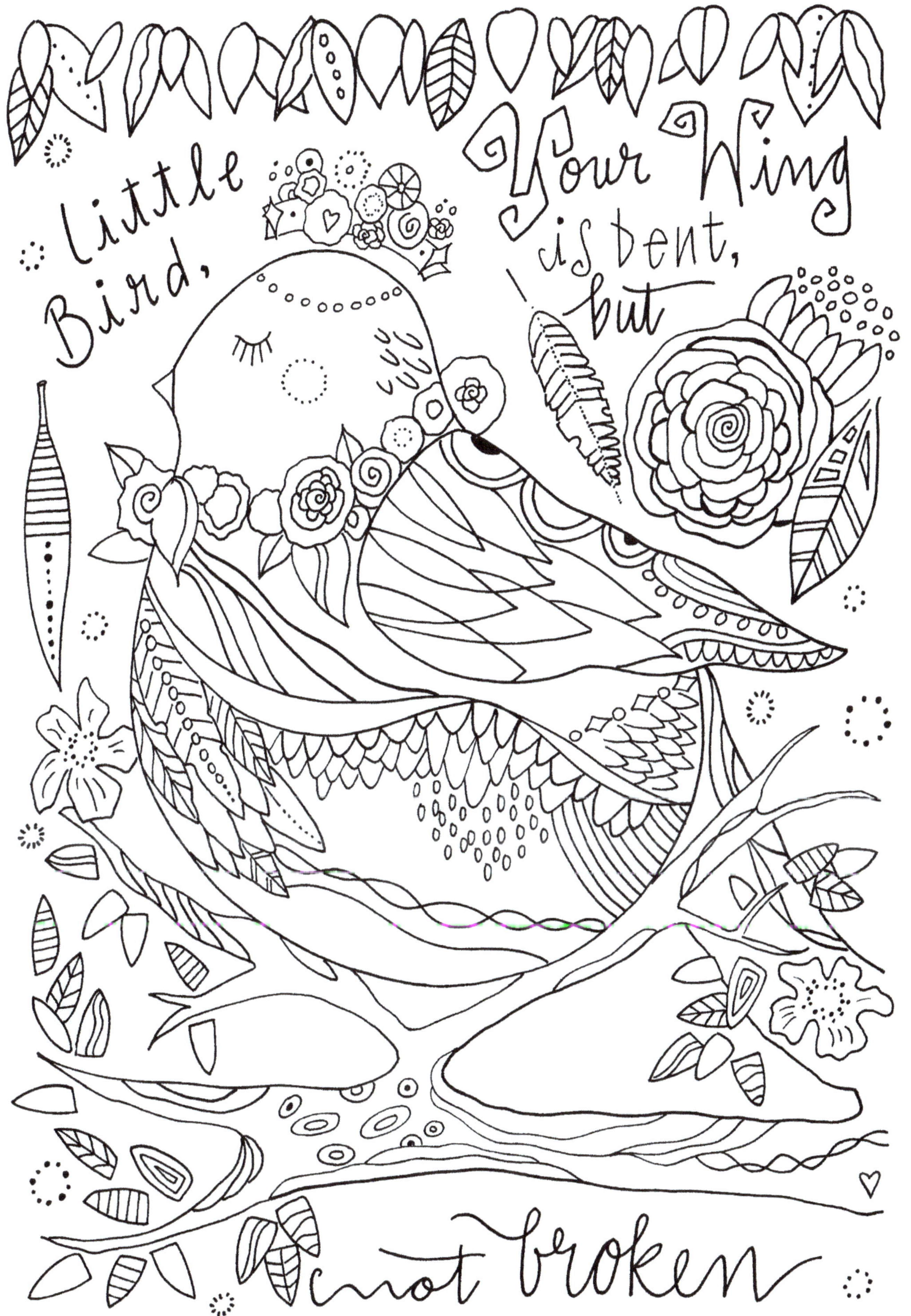
Little Bird,
Your Wing
is bent,
but
not broken

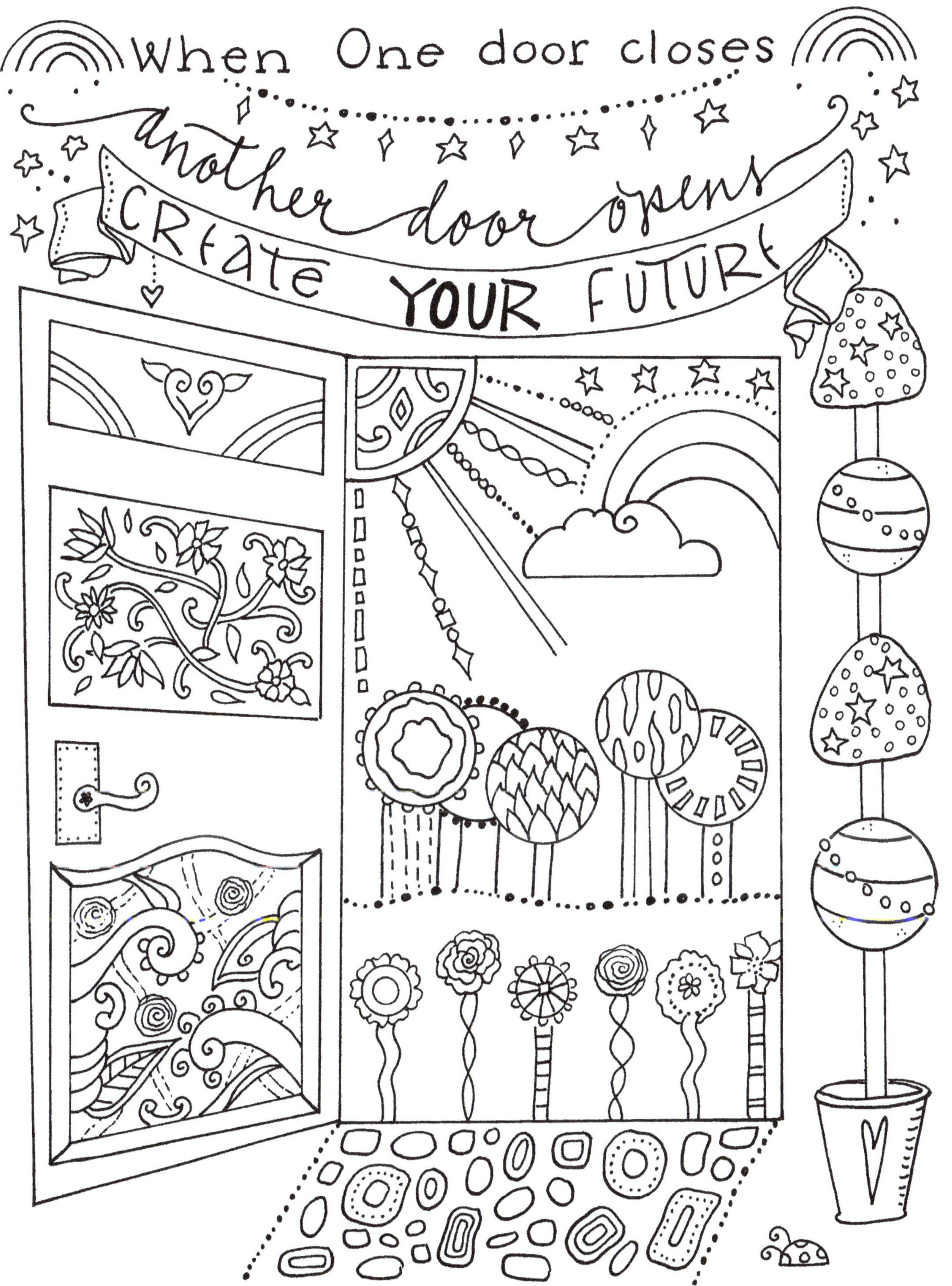
When One door closes
another door opens
CREATE YOUR FUTURE

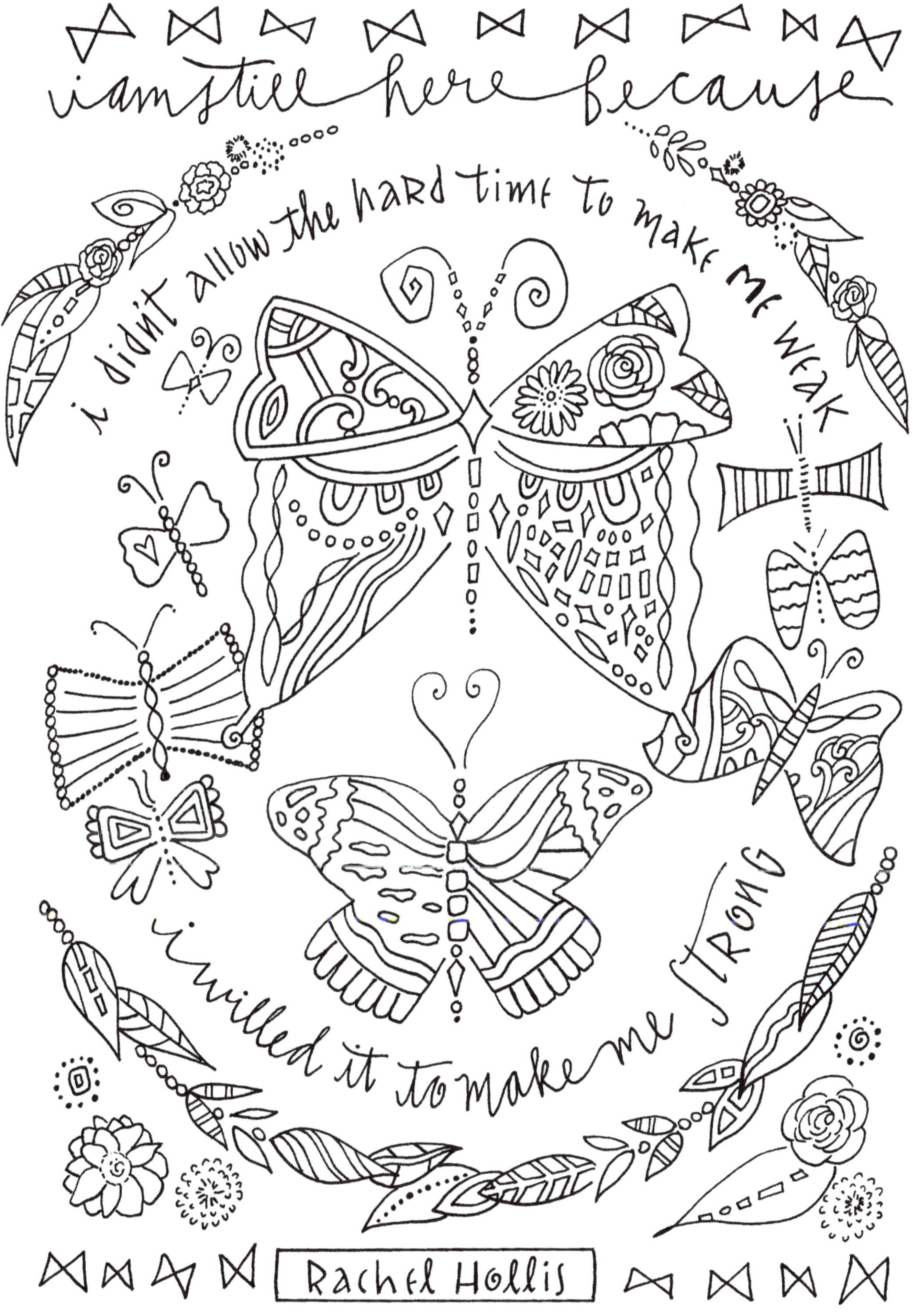
i am still here because
i didn't allow the hard time to make me weak
i willed it to make me strong
Rachel Hollis

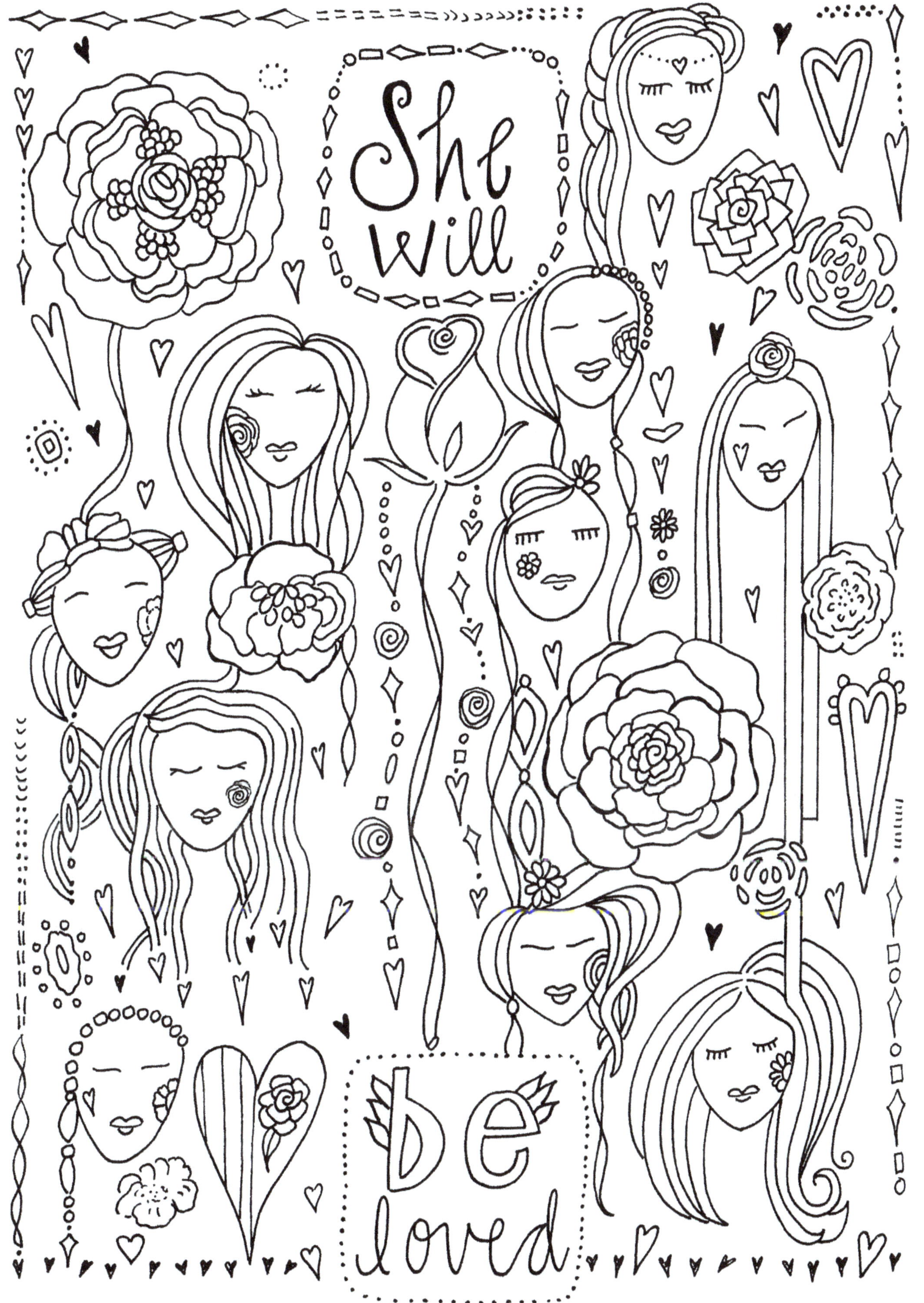
She will
be loved

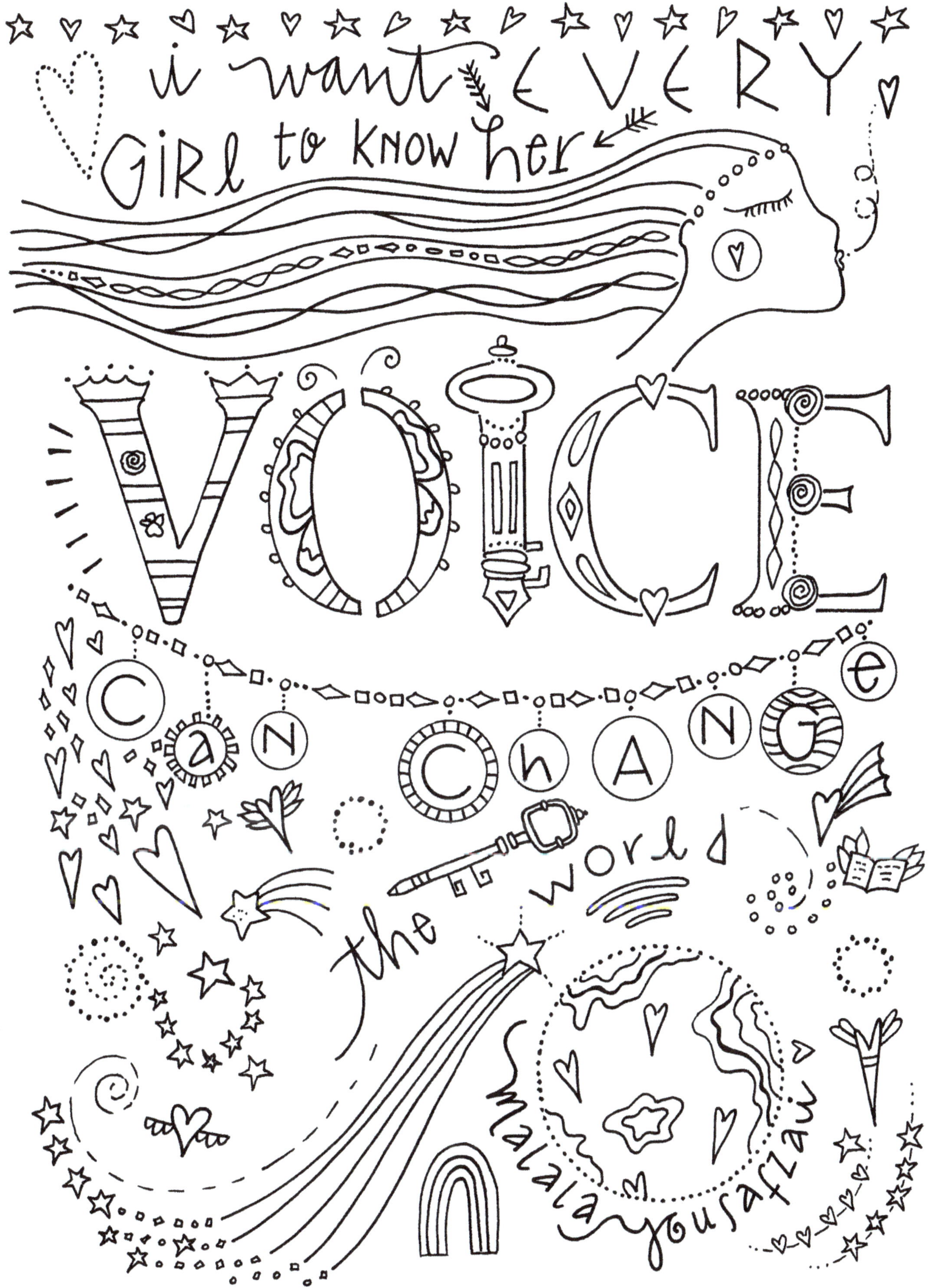
i want EVERY
GirL to KNOW her
VOICE
can change
the world
Malala Yousafzai

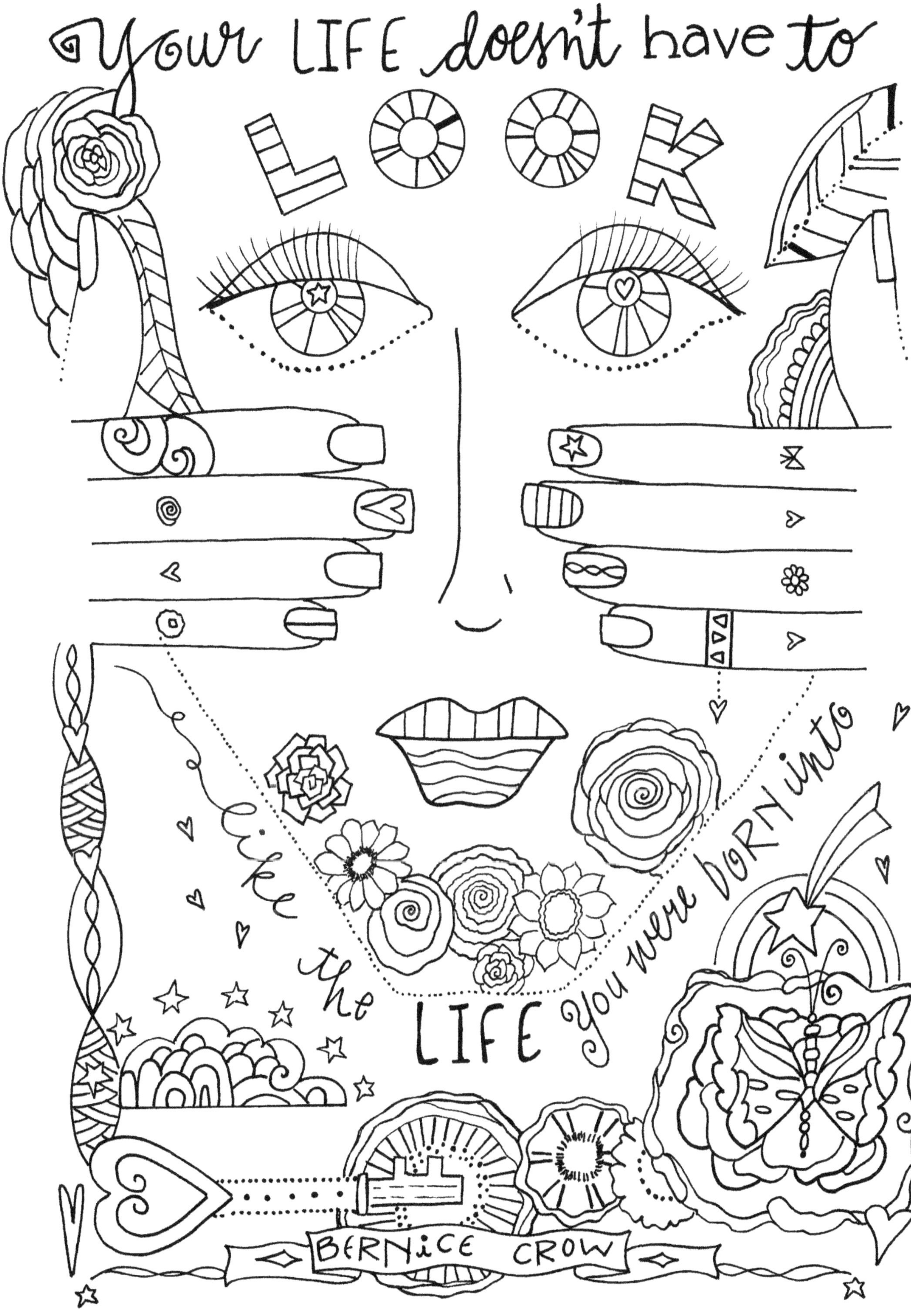

Your LIFE doesn't have to

LOOK

like the LIFE you were BORN into

BERNICE CROW

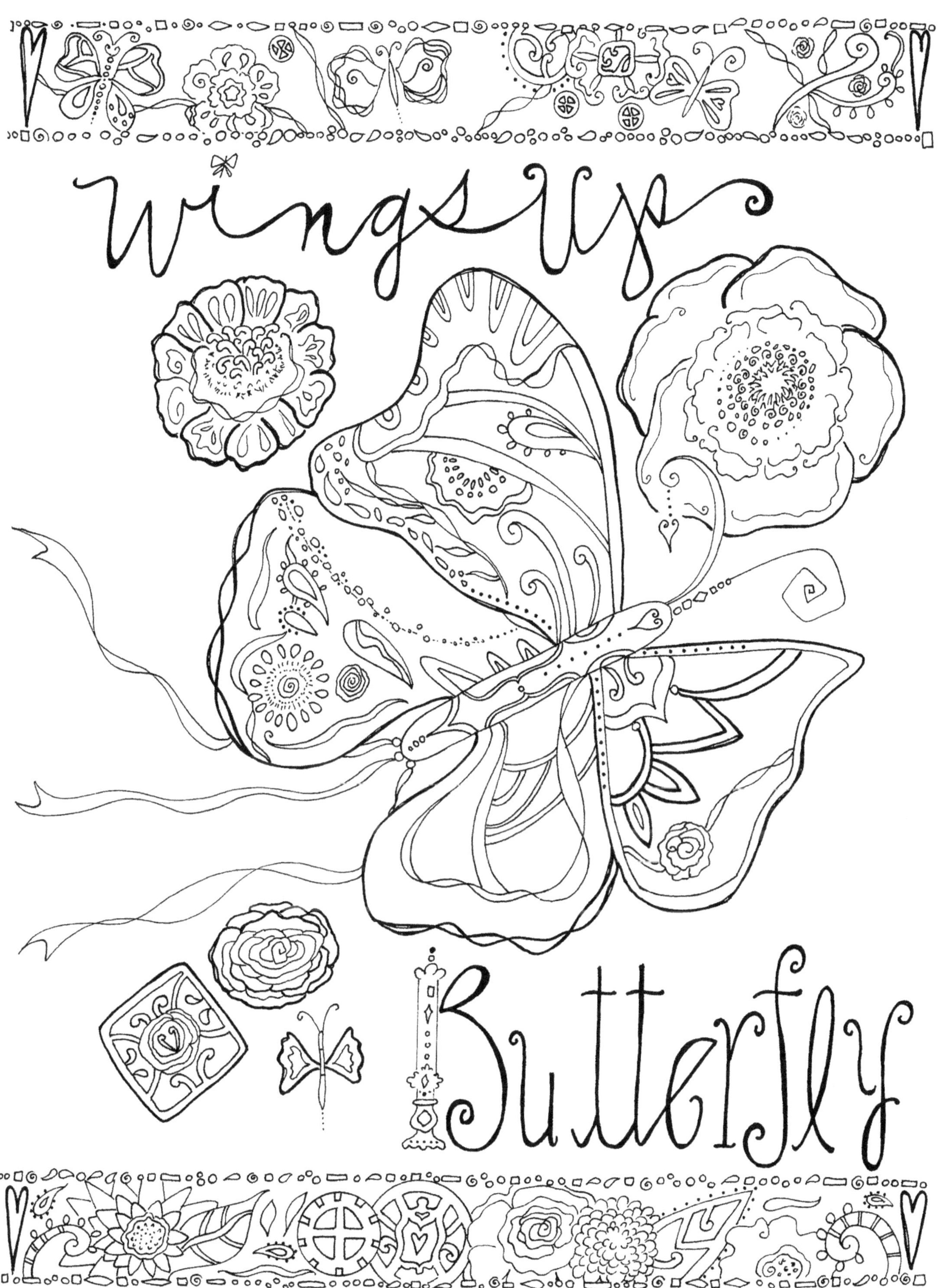
Wings Up
Butterfly

Love is patient love is kind. It does NOT envy, it does not boast, it is not proud. It does not dishonor others, it is not self-seeking, it is not easily angered, it keeps no record of wrongs. Love does not delight in evil but rejoices with the truth. It always protects, always trusts, always hopes, always perseveres. Love never fails.

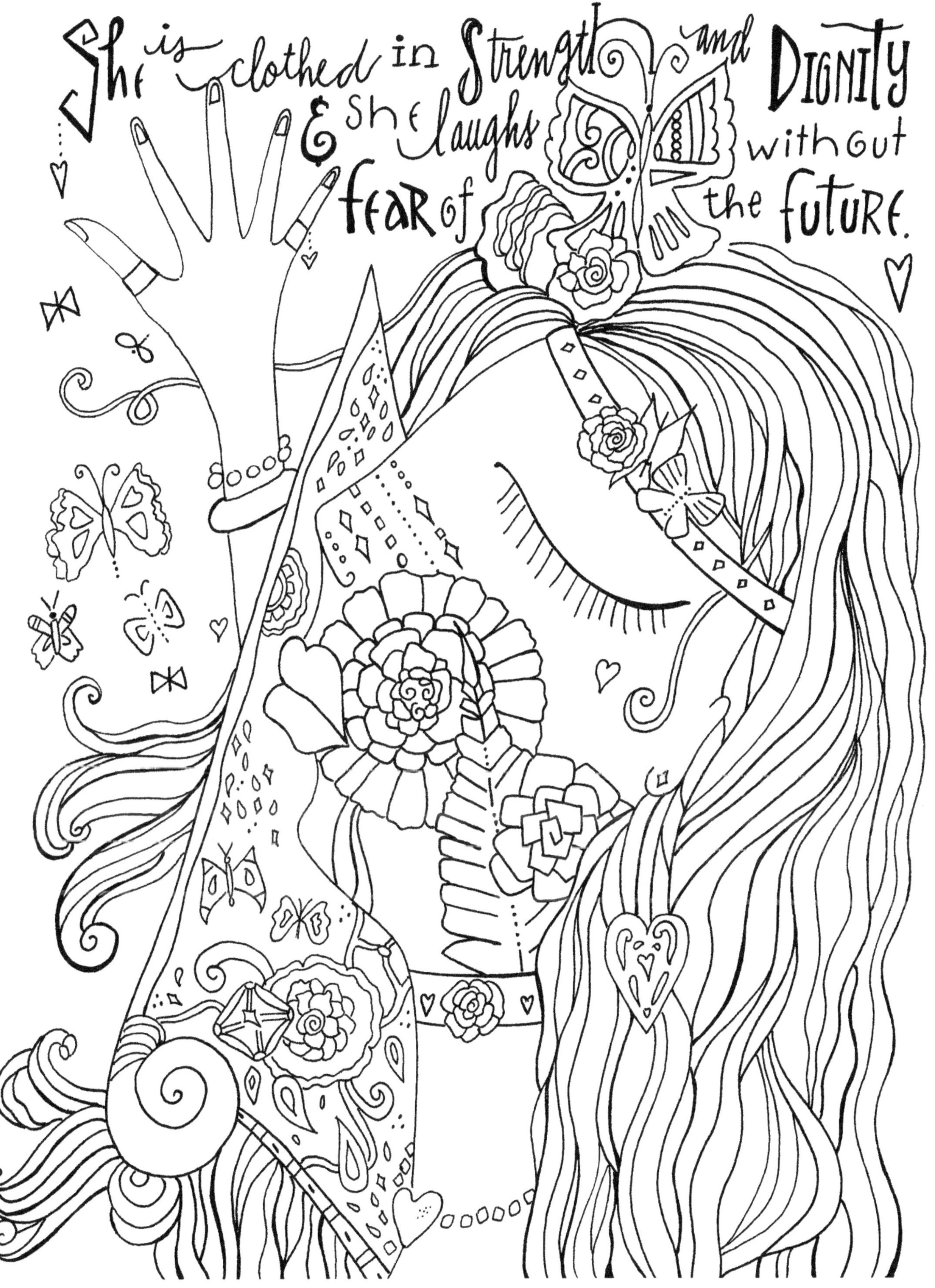
She is clothed in Strength and Dignity
& She laughs without
fear of the future.

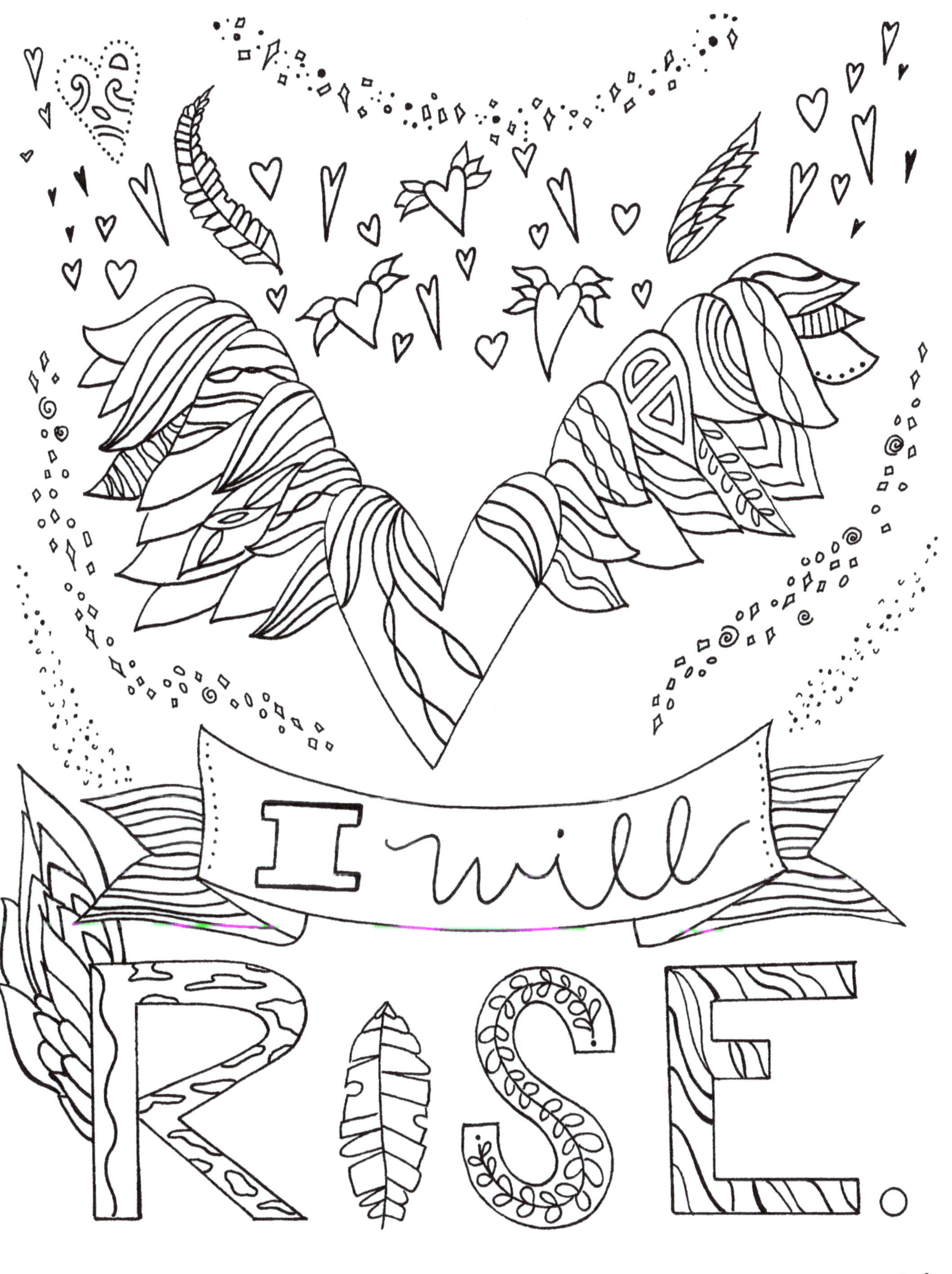

I will
RISE.

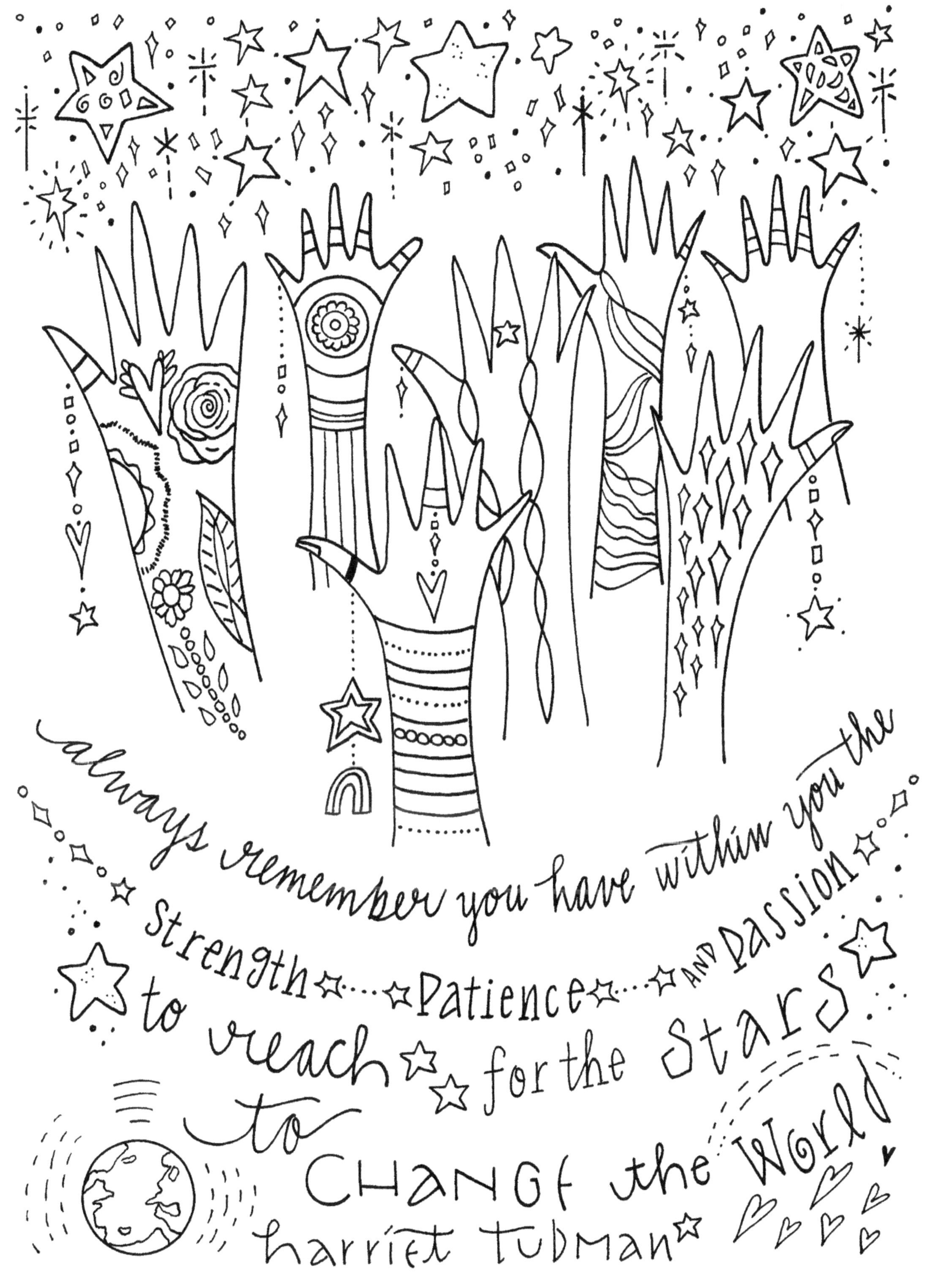
always remember you have within you the
strength patience and passion
to reach for the stars
to
change the world
harriet tubman

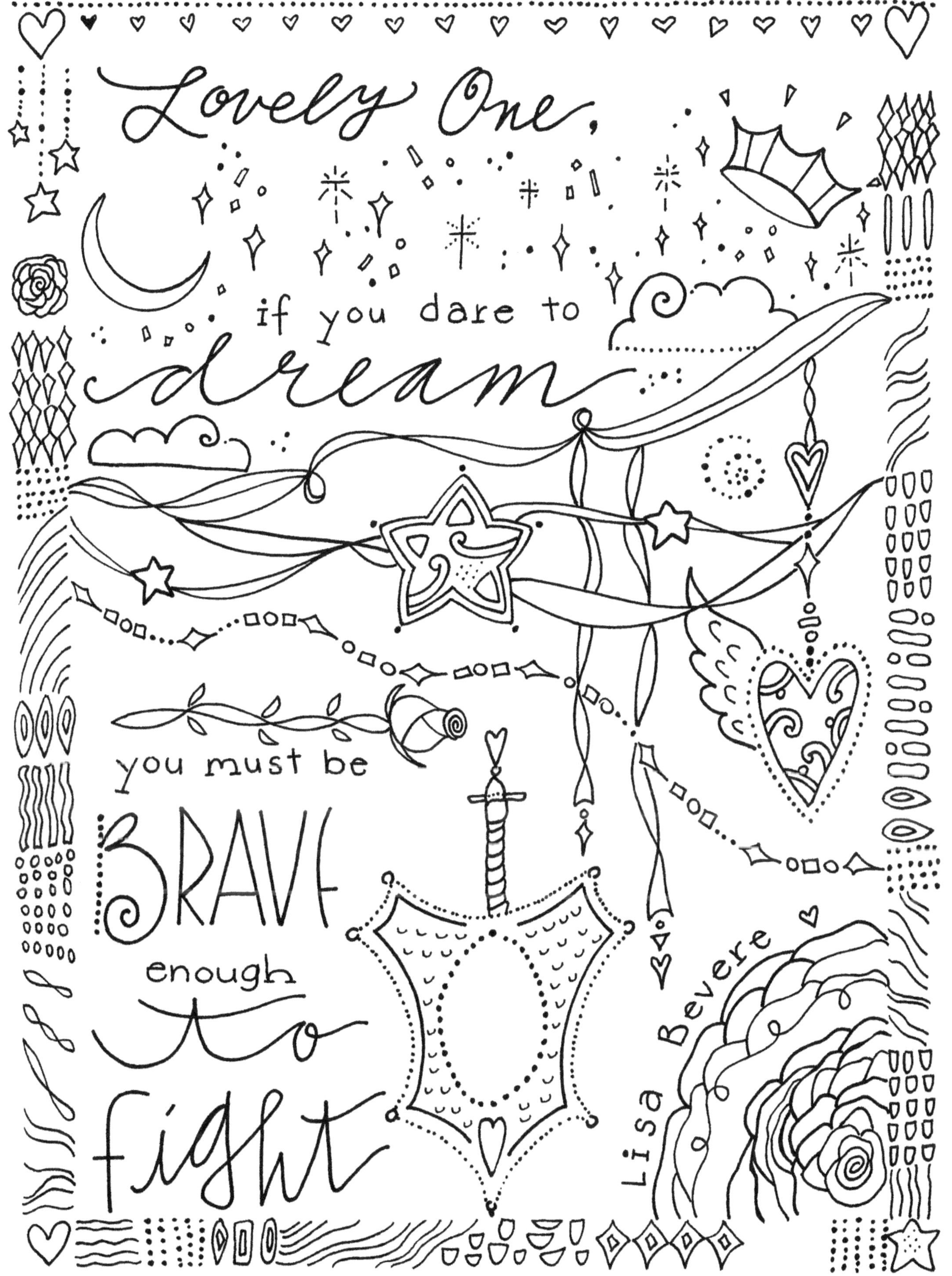
Lovely One,
if you dare to
dream
you must be
BRAVE
enough
to
fight
Lisa Bevere

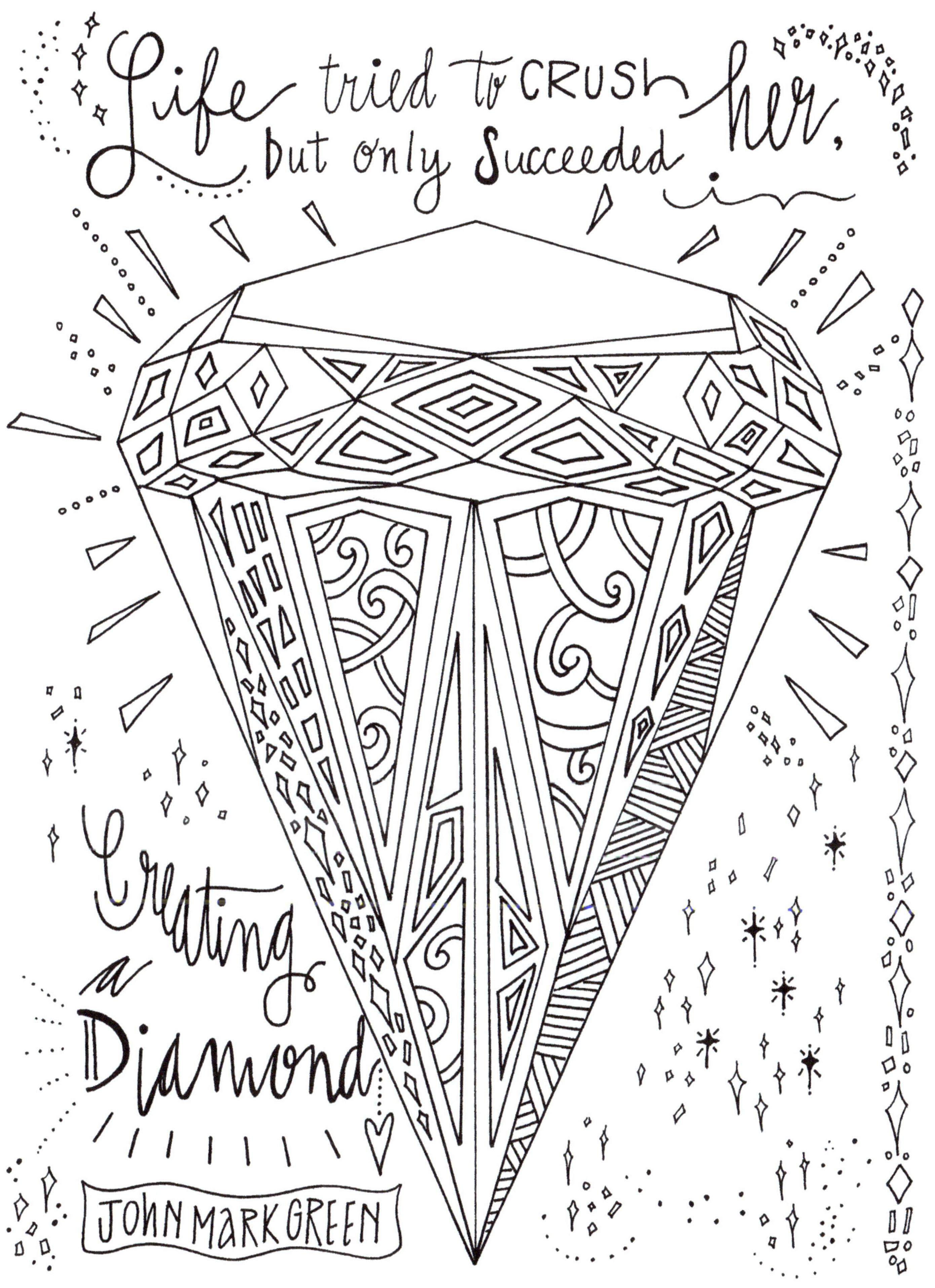
Life tried to crush her,
but only succeeded in
Creating a Diamond
JOHN MARK GREEN

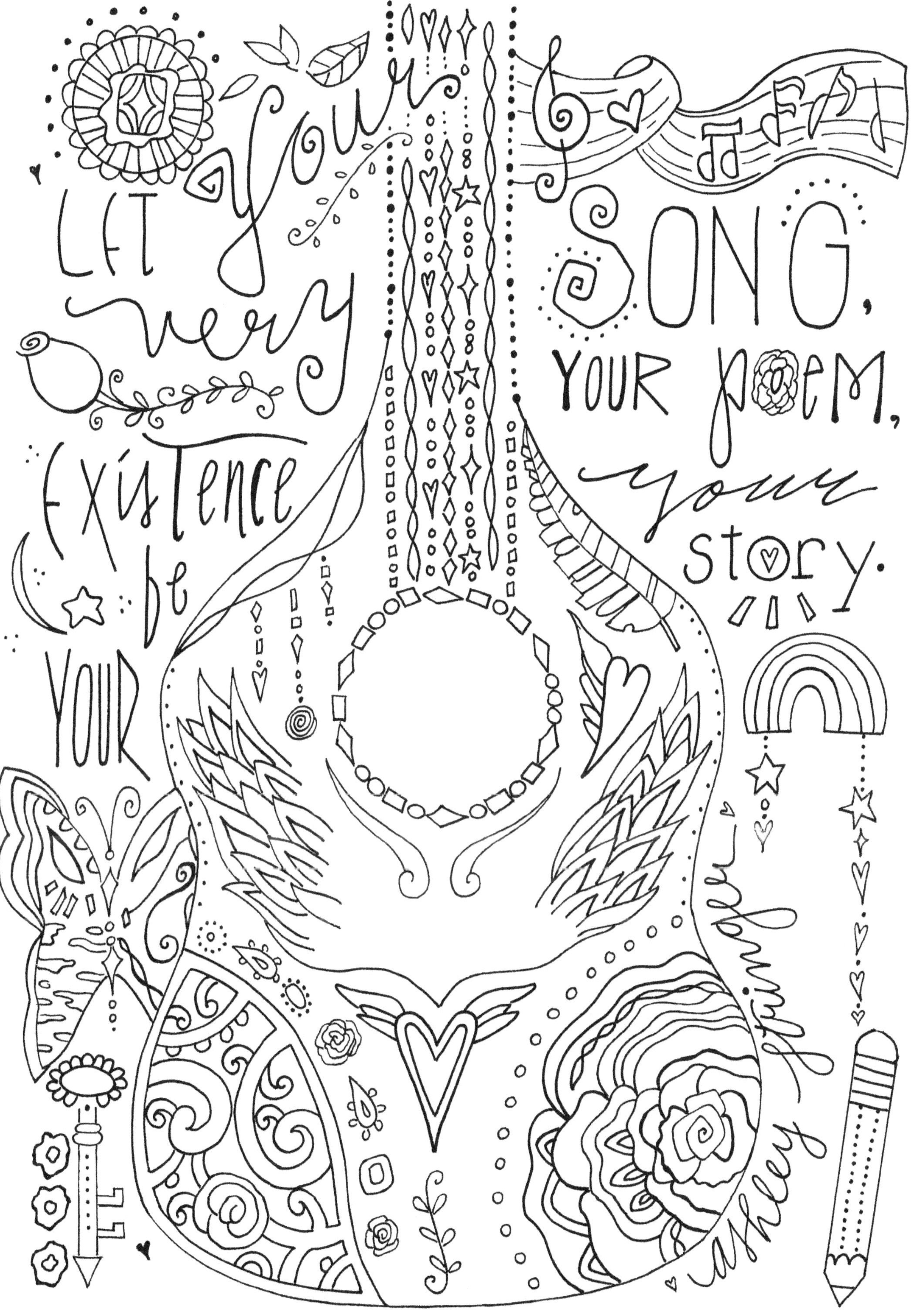
LET your very existence be your SONG, YOUR poem, your story.
ashley frimpong

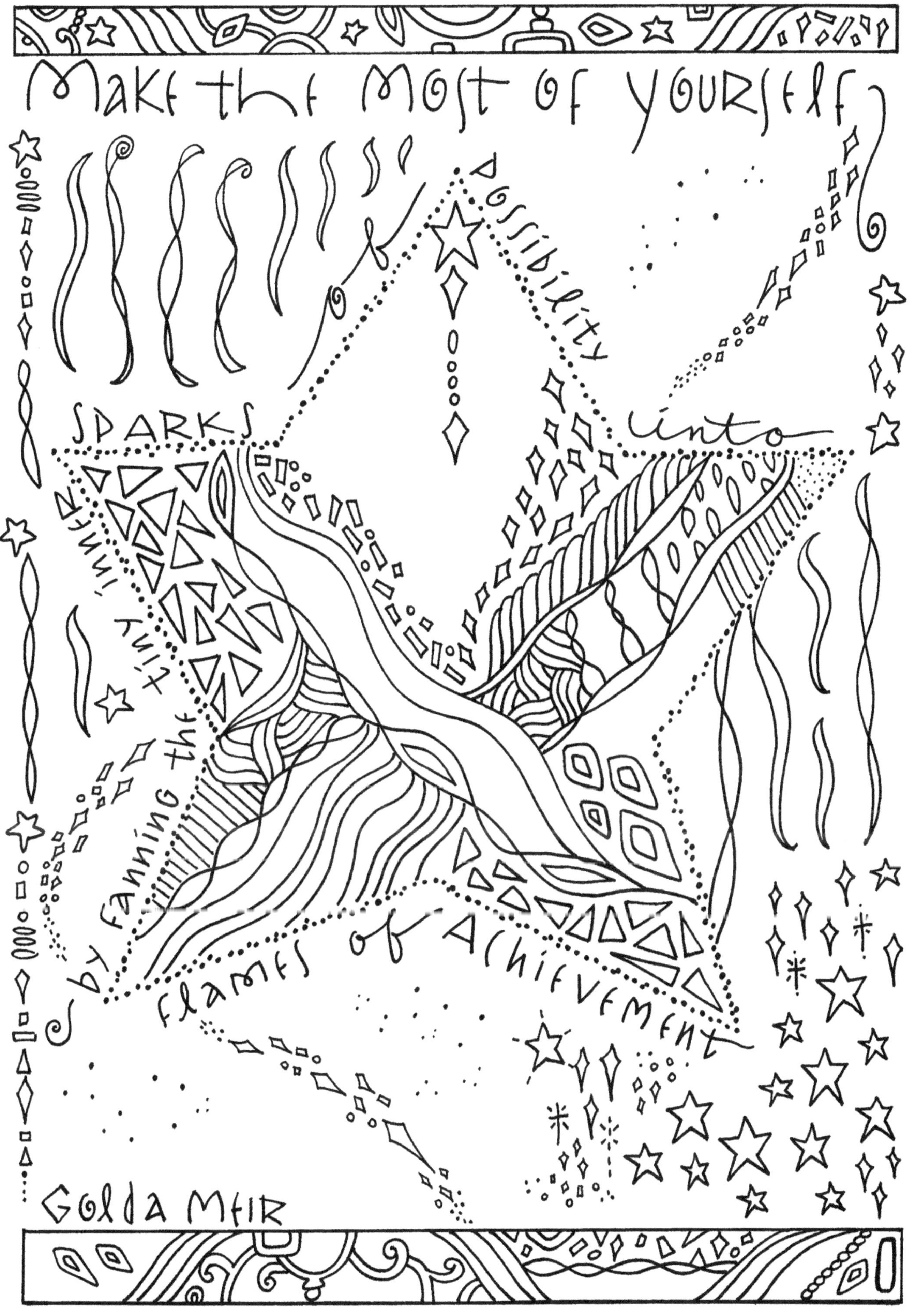
Make the Most of yourself
by fanning the tiny, inner sparks of possibility into flames of achievement
Golda Meir

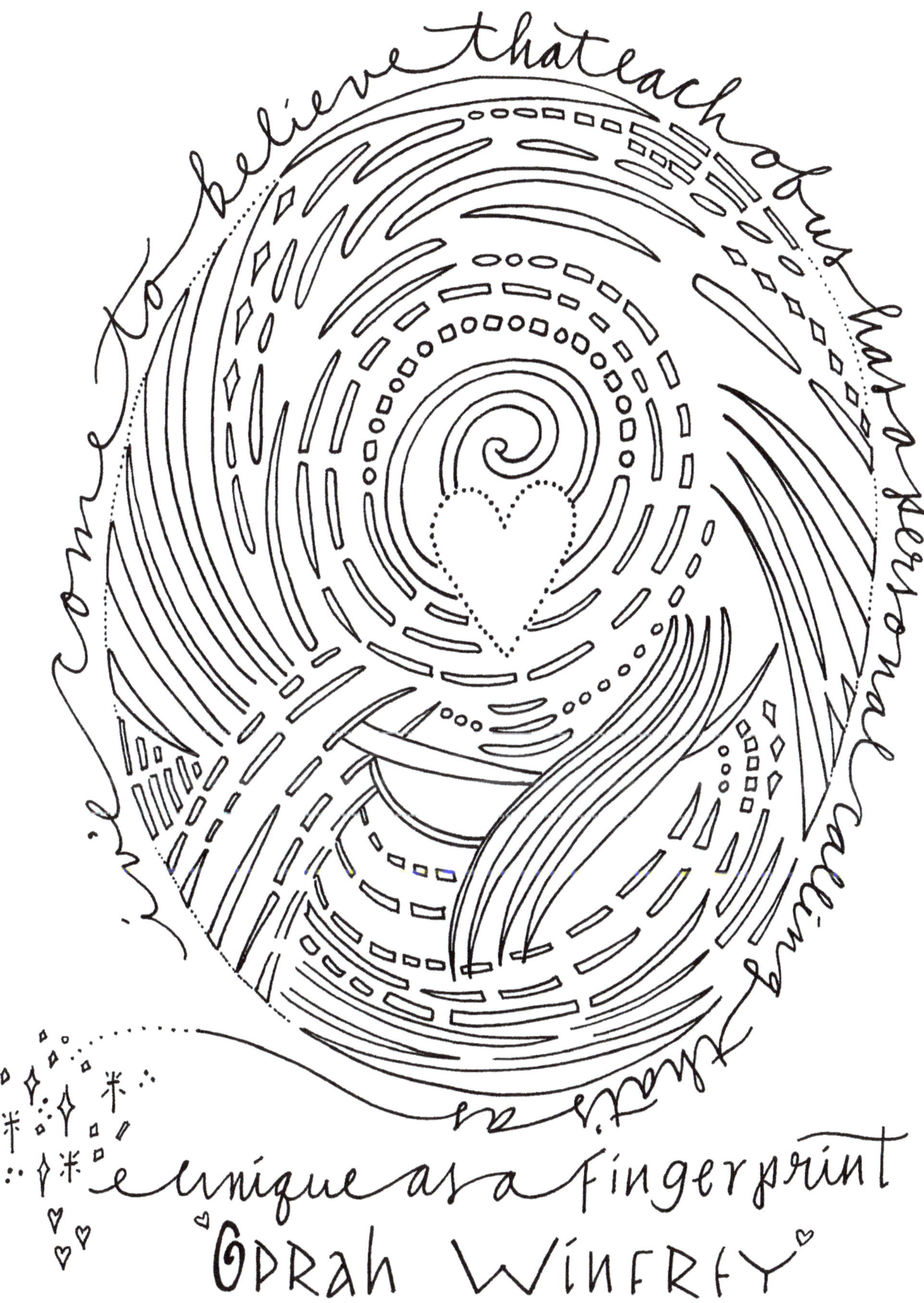
I've come to believe that each of us has a personal calling that's as unique as a fingerprint
Oprah Winfrey

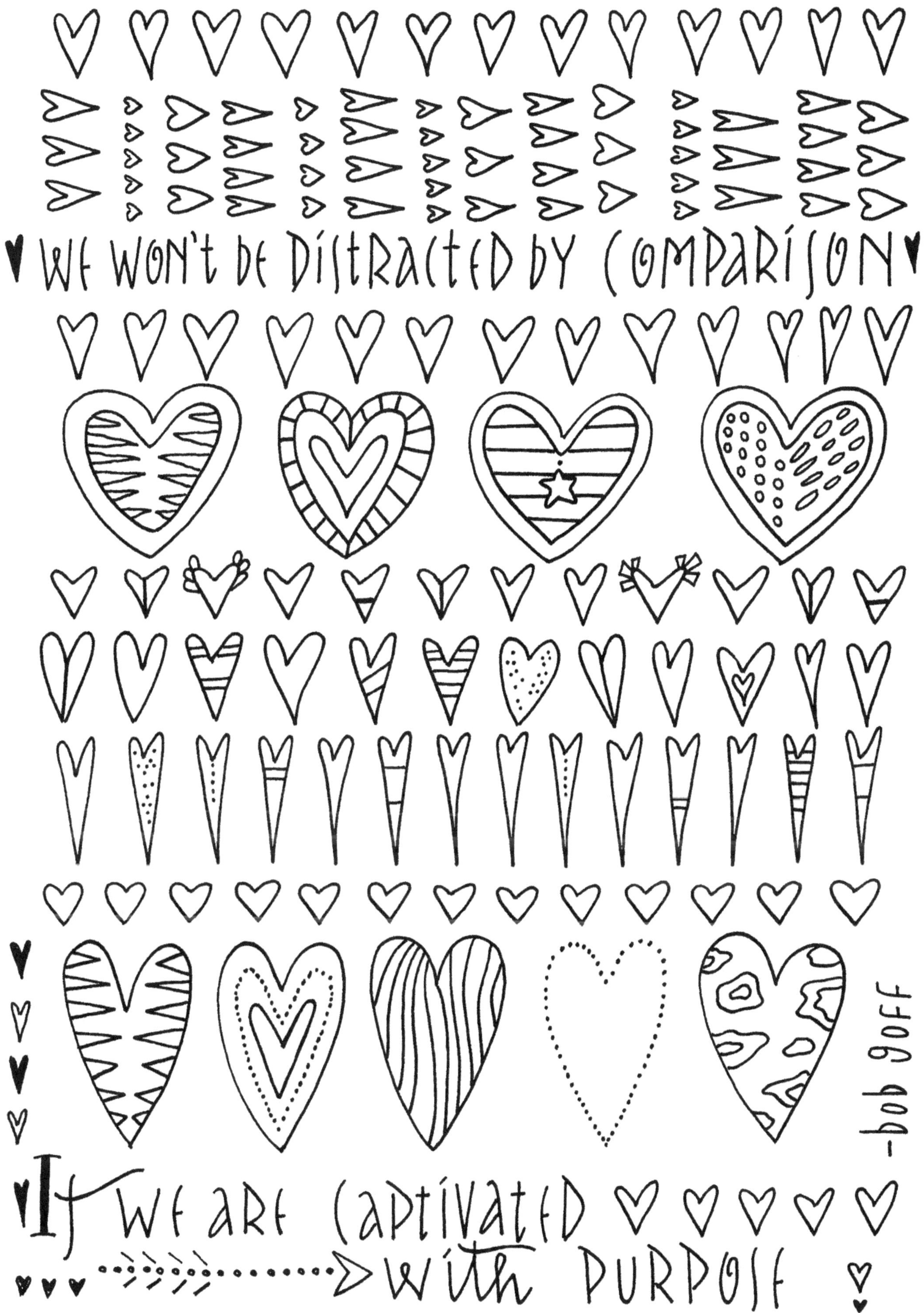
We won't be distracted by comparison
If we are captivated with purpose
-bob goff

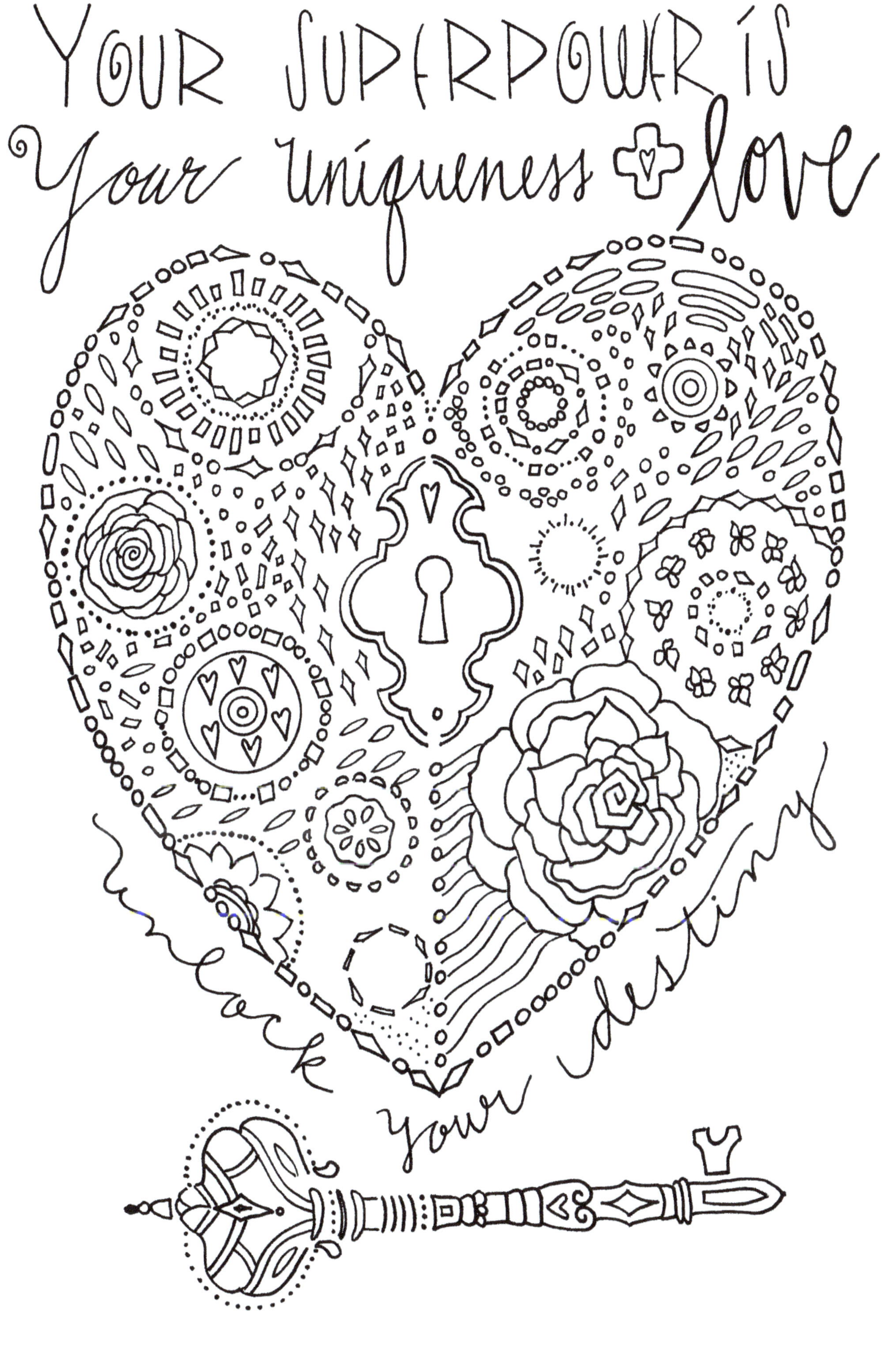

YOUR SUPERPOWER IS

Your Uniqueness + love

unlock your destiny

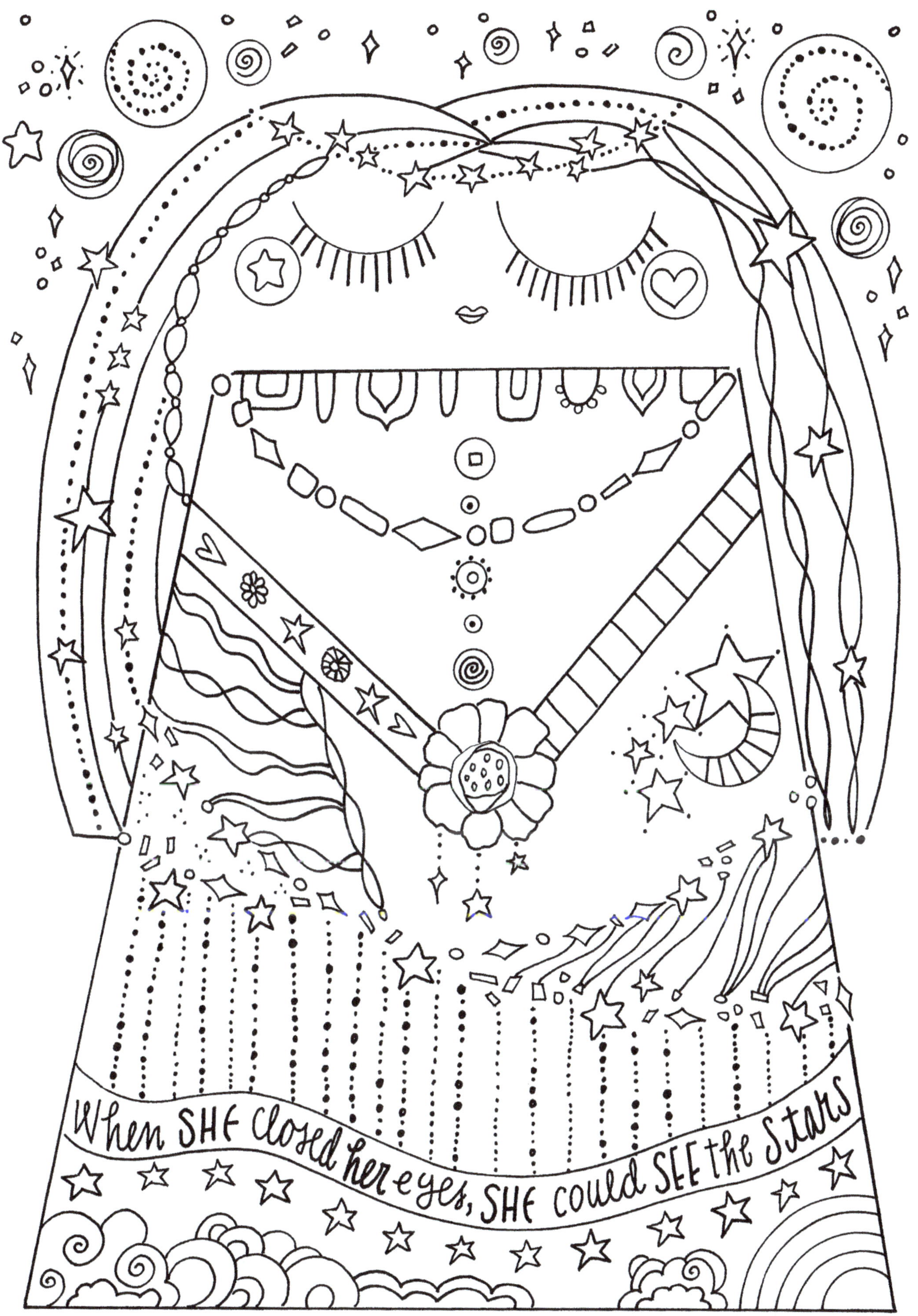
When SHE closed her eyes, SHE could SEE the Stars

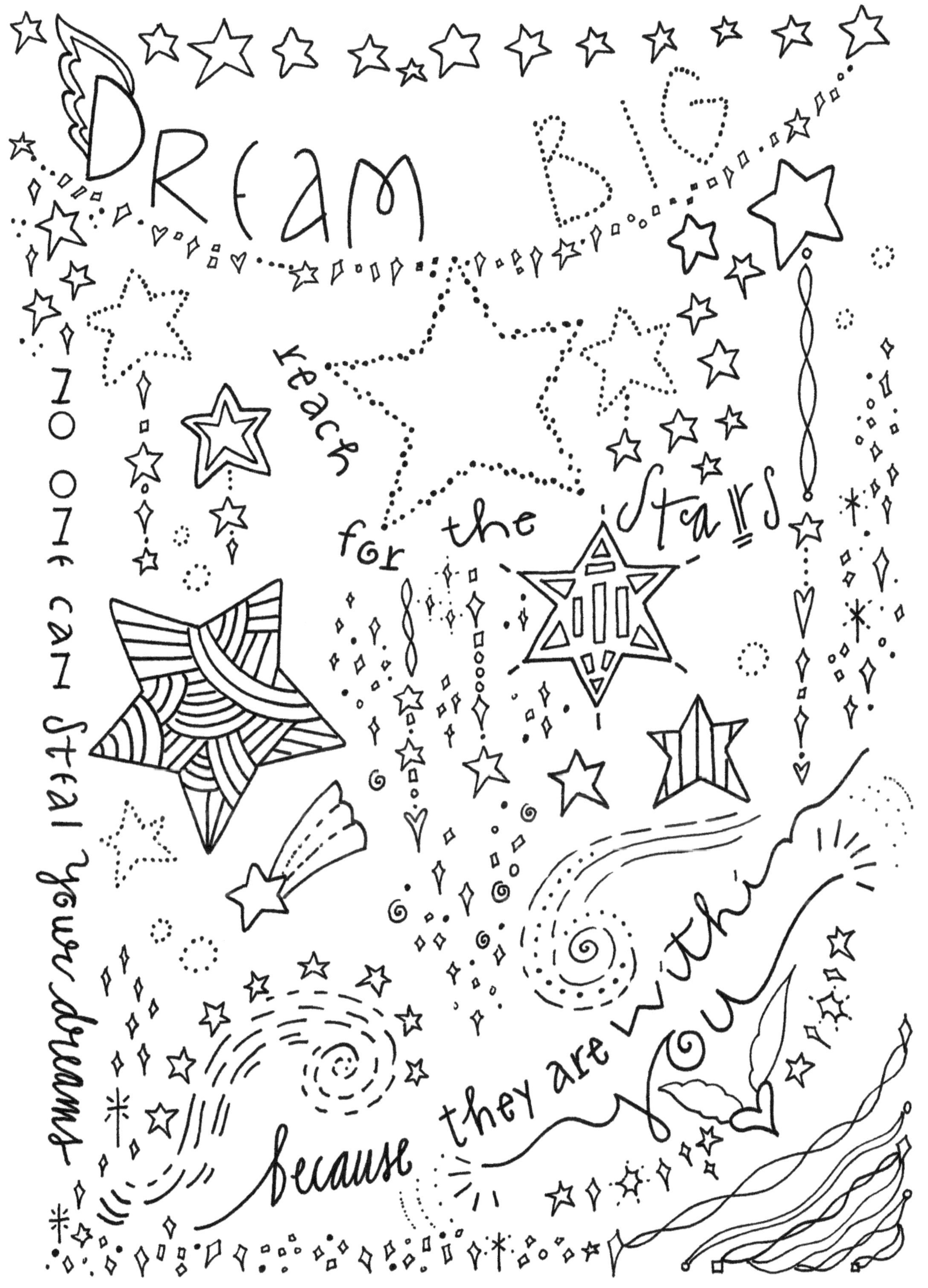

DREAM BIG
reach for the stars
no one can steal your dreams
because they are within you

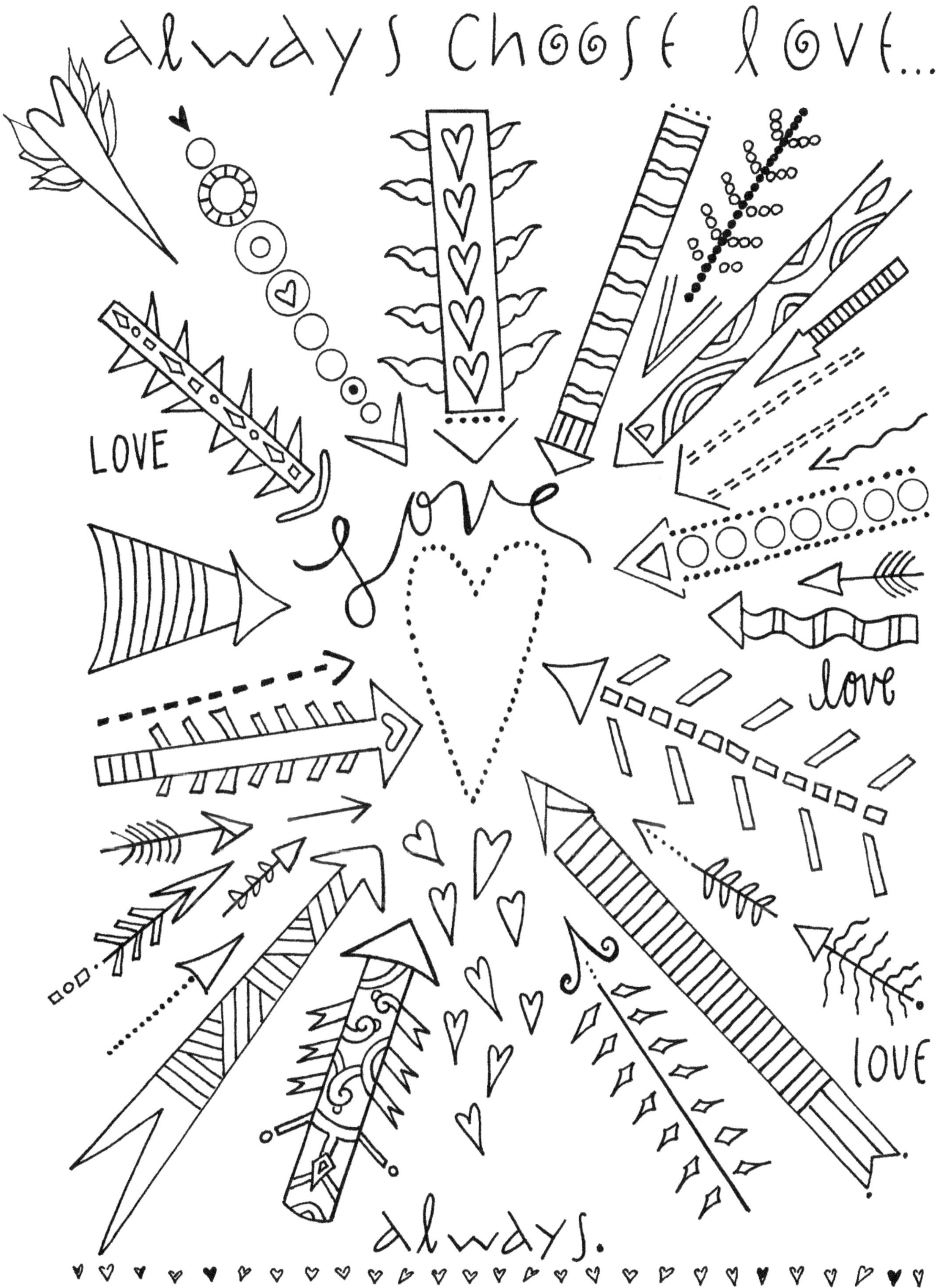
always choose love...
LOVE
love
love
LOVE
always.

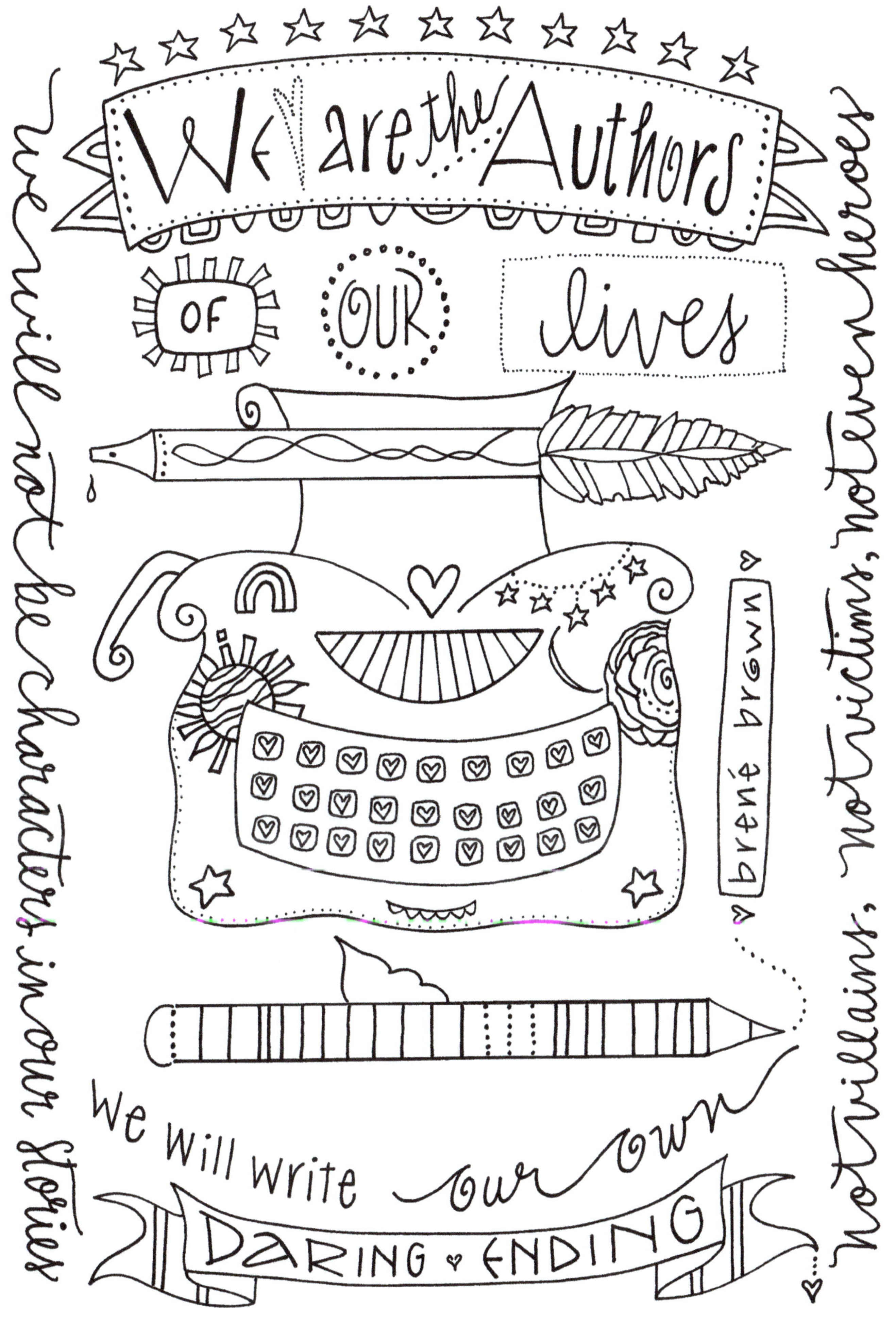
We are the Authors
of
OUR
lives
we will not be characters in our stories
not heroes, not even villains, not victims,
brené brown
We will write our own
DARING ENDING

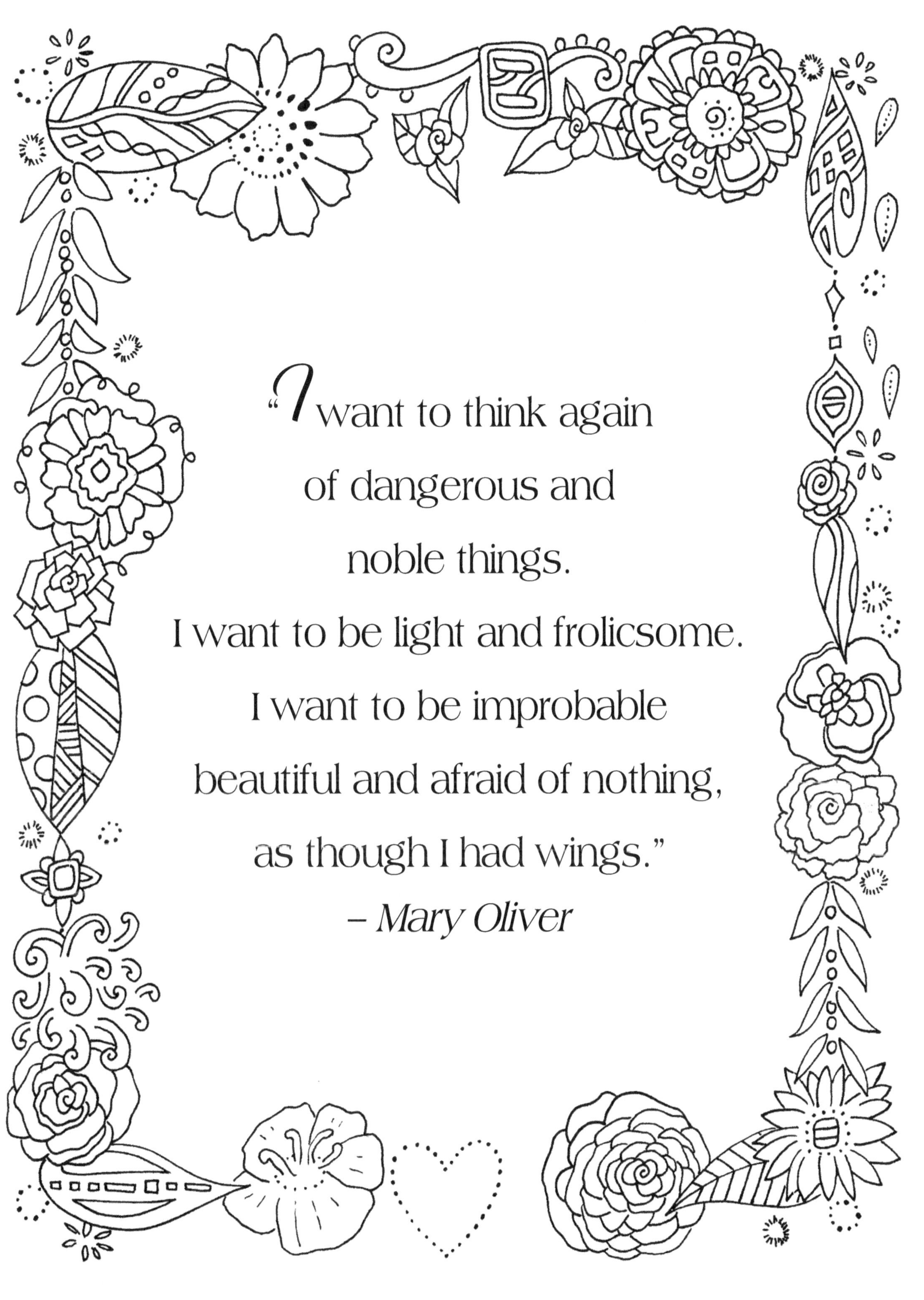
"I want to think again
of dangerous and
noble things.
I want to be light and frolicsome.
I want to be improbable
beautiful and afraid of nothing,
as though I had wings."
– *Mary Oliver*

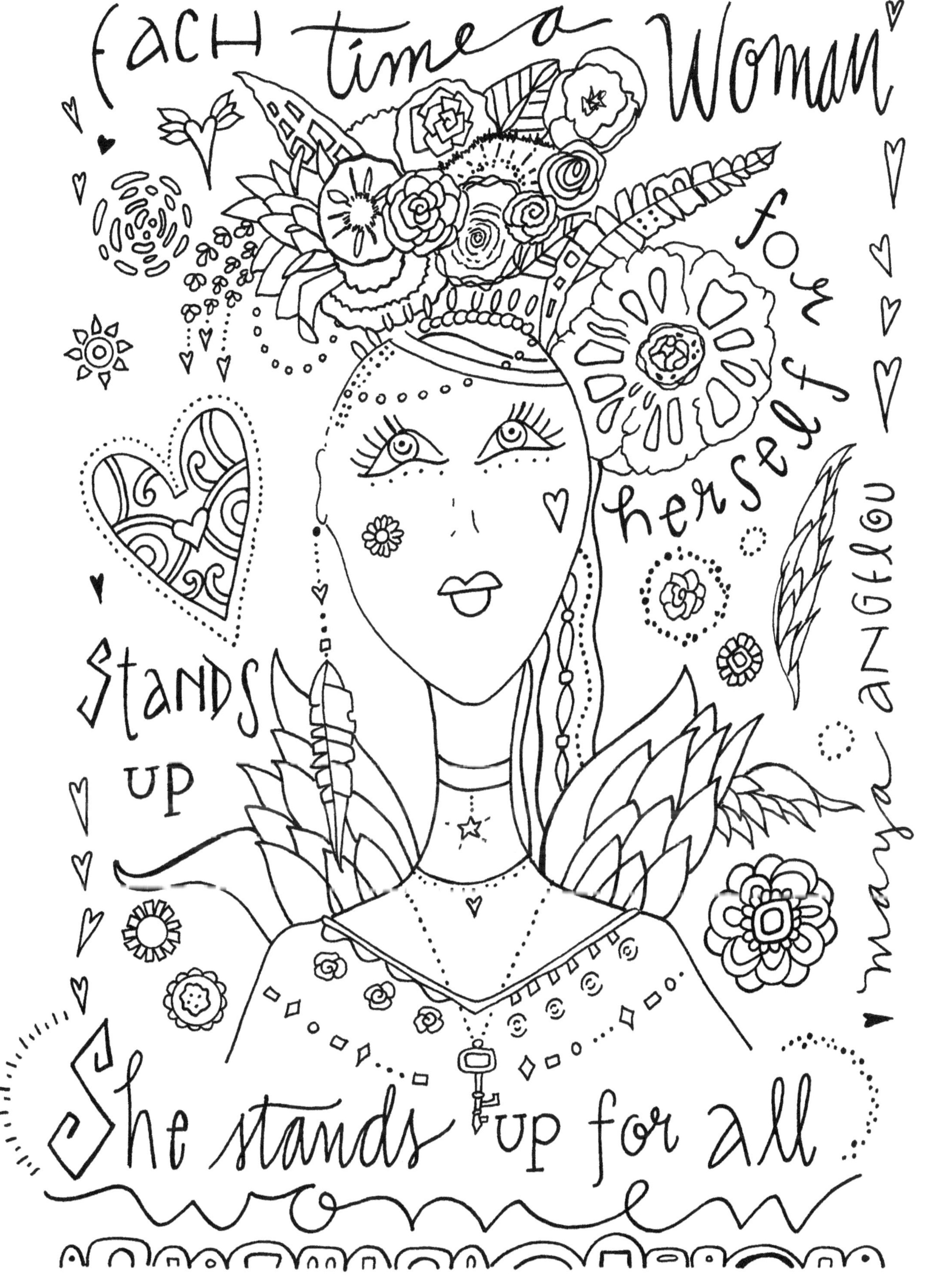
Each time a Woman
Stands up
for herself
She stands up for all
maya angelou

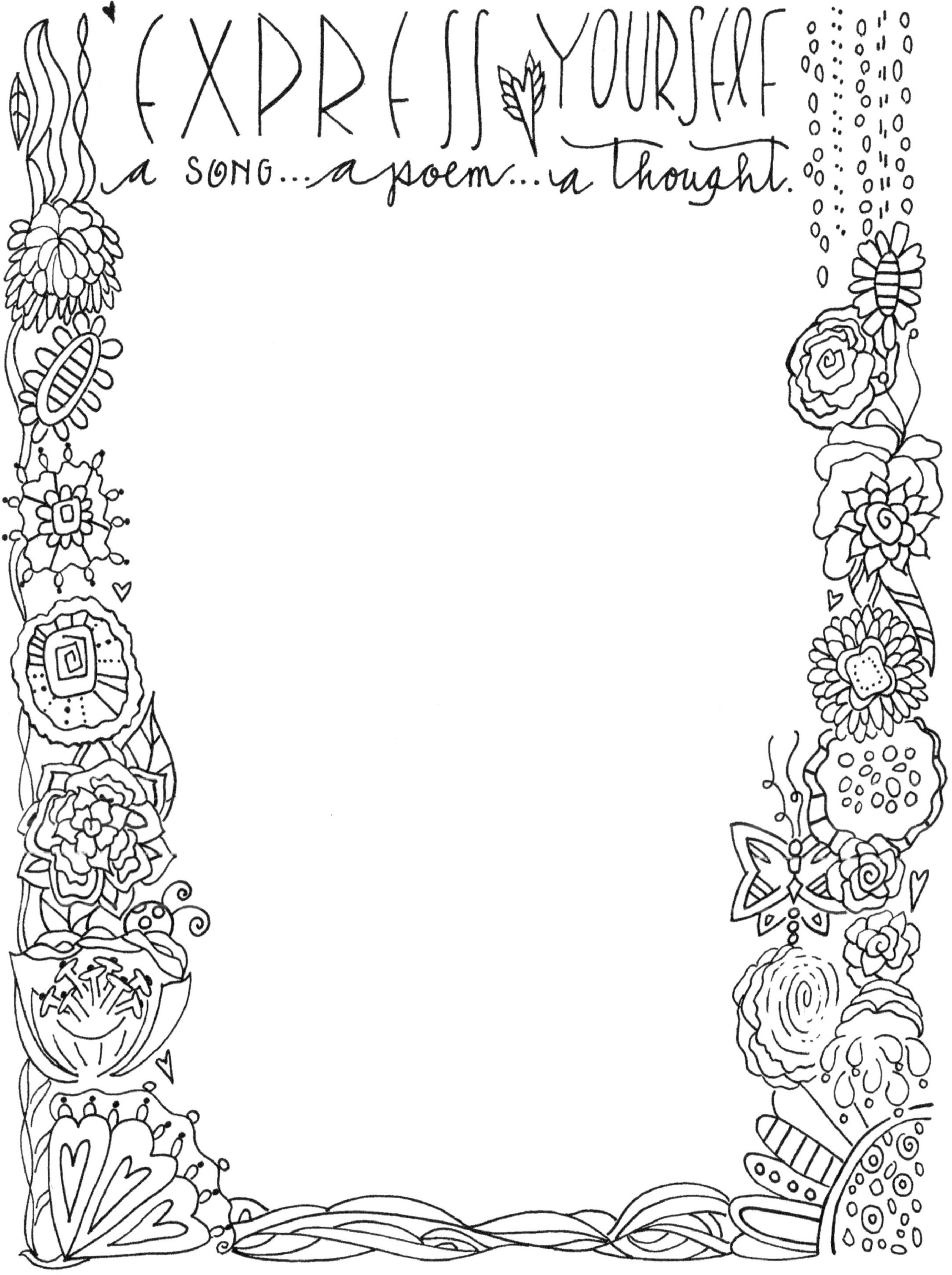
EXPRESS YOURSELF
a song... a poem... a thought.

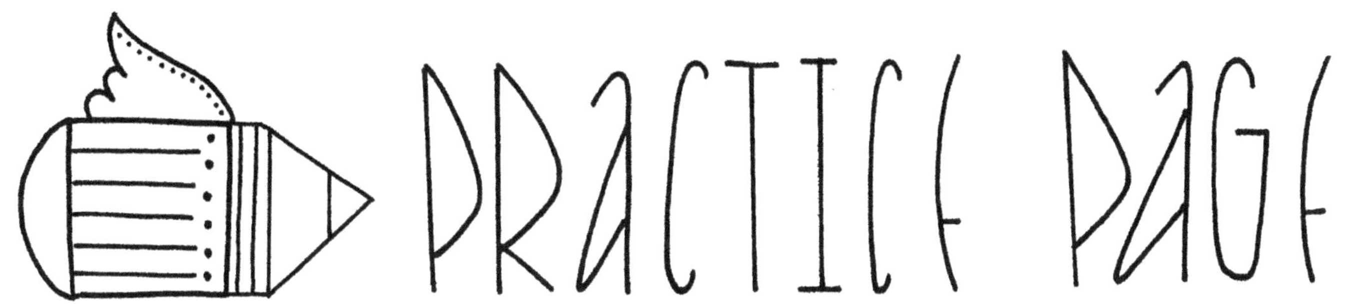
PRACTICE PAGE

A Little About April...

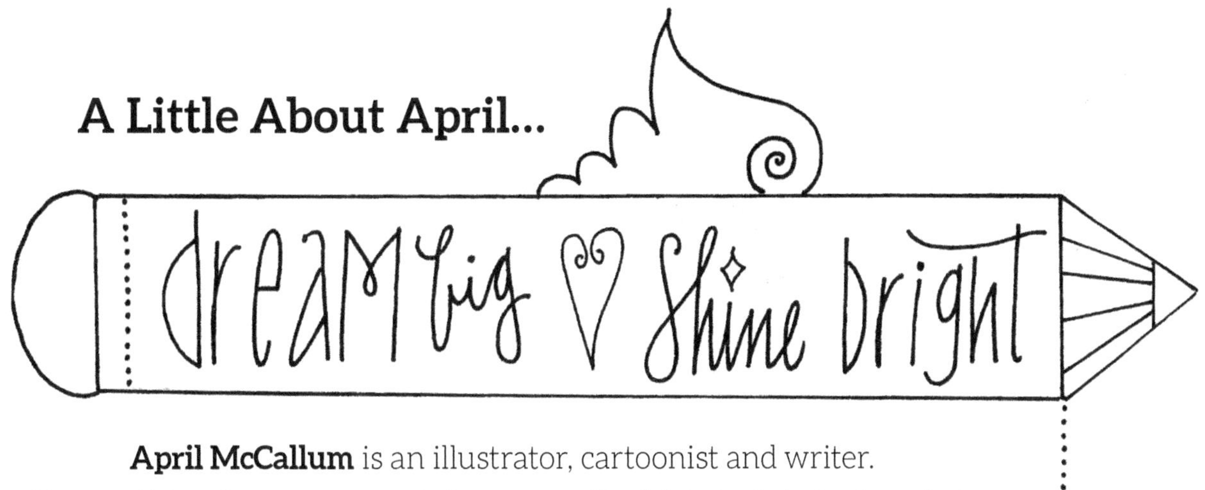

April McCallum is an illustrator, cartoonist and writer. Since retiring from a successful career in the high-tech industry, she's focused her creative passions on art, writing and advocacy projects. Her artwork has been licensed and featured on magazine covers, for business and non-profits, and on a variety of gift products. Her writing and artwork has appeared in a variety of magazines and featured on CNBC. Her signature style combines words and visuals, color and design. Her writing and illustration work is inspirational, hope-filled and empowering, while her cartoonist side brings a unique twist of humor to the table.

April has long been an advocacy artist designing creative pieces that interweave words and visuals to speak to issues close to her heart. Current topics include empowering women, adoption, grief and loss, breast cancer awareness, addiction and the power of one.

COLORS OF HOPE: Breast Cancer Warriors Coloring Book
REFLECTIONS OF LOVE: Coloring Book Therapy for Grief & Loss
BRAVE WINGS: A Coloring Book to Celebrate & Empower Women

Pete Berg and April McCallum have been creative collaborators on a variety of colorful and interesting projects over the years. If you would like to connect with Pete Berg regarding a graphic art project, he can be reached at: ohberg3@gmail.com

Website: www.aprilmccallumdesigns.com
Email: april@aprilmccallumdesigns.com
Blog: DestinysWomen.com
Facebook: @AprilMcCallumDesigns
Instagram: @AprilCartoons | @AprilLovesColor | @PinkCartoons
Twitter: @AprilCartoons | @PinkCartoons
Pinterest: https://www.pinterest.com/aprilmccallum/
https://www.pinterest.com/pinkpassionlife/

www.ingramcontent.com/pod-product-compliance
Lightning Source LLC
LaVergne TN
LVHW061251100826
845148LV00008B/1091

* 9 7 8 1 7 3 2 5 7 5 2 5 7 *